The ULTIMATE TISSUE TOPPER COLLECTION

Edited by Vicki Blizzard

Editor: Vicki Blizzard
Associate Editor: Tanya Turner
Art Director: Brad Snow
Technical Editor: June Sprunger
Copy Editor: Michelle Beck

Photography: Andy J. Burnfield, Scott Campbell
Photo Stylists: Martha Coquat

Publishing Services Manager: Brenda Gallmeyer
Graphic Arts Supervisor/Artist: Ronda Bechinski
Cover Design: Brad Snow
Book Design: Amy S. Lin
Production Assistants: Marj Morgan
Technical Artists: June Sprunger, Chad Summers
Traffic Coordinator: Sandra Beres

Chief Executive Officer: John Robinson
Publishing Director: David McKee
Book Marketing Director: Craig Scott
Editorial Director: Vivian Rothe

Library of Congress Number: 2003100405
ISBN: 1-57367-133-9
First Printing: 2004
Printed in China

Visit us at
NeedlecraftShop.com

Every effort has been made to ensure the accuracy and completeness of the
instructions in this book. However, we cannot be responsible for human
error or for the results when using materials other than those specified in
the instructions, or for variations in individual work.

2 3 4 5 6 7 8 9

A Note From The Editor

Tissue box covers are my favorite project to stitch. I love being able to change the look of such an ordinary household item into a decorator piece or a whimsical accent, depending on my mood of the week.

We've arranged the chapters of this book by rooms in a home. Don't feel limited by the location of projects in a particular chapter, though—feel free to stitch one of the sophisticated covers in the dining room chapter, for example, to place in an elegant powder room. Or if you love vibrant hues and whimsical motifs, stitch one of the kids' room toppers to put in your living room for a touch of bright color and warm smiles.

Tissue toppers also make perfect gifts for housewarmings, anniversaries, new jobs and hostess gifts! What person wouldn't love to receive a hand-stitched gift that can be displayed in their home or office every day of the year?

If you're anything like me, you get attached to a certain brand of tissues because of the pretty boxes that perfectly match your bathroom, bedroom or kitchen, only to have that design discontinued and replaced with something in the wrong color. With this collection of toppers, you'll always have just the right accent to coordinate with any room of your home.

I hope you find many favorites in the pages of this book and that you have as much fun stitching these projects as our staff and designers did in putting the book together for you!

Happy stitching!

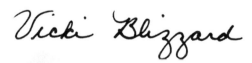

Contents

The Kitchen

Checks & Cherries. 7
To Market 9
A Spot of Tea 12
Ruler of the Roost 13
Kitty Chef 15
Apple Delight 17
Garden Bees. 20
Sunflower Gingham 22
Tropical Treat. 23

The Family Room

Tribal Motif 30
Pastel Patchwork 31
Woven Lattice 32
God Bless This Home 35
Southwestern Quilt 36
End Table Organizer. 38
My Favorite Things 41
Old Glory Quilt Block. 44
New Mexico. 47
Missing Pieces 48

The Living Room

Victorian Elegance 52
Golden Diamonds 53
Diagonal Weave 54
Art Deco. 57
Southwest Quilt Block. 58
Silver Filigree 60
Satin & Gold 63
Stenciled Flowers 64

The Dining Room

Sweet Sunflower 67
Patchwork Pinwheels. 68
Elegant Fruit Basket 69
Cross Stitch Fantasy. 70
Study in Blue. 72
Elegant Plaid 73
English Cottage. 74

The Bathroom

Stylized Flowers 82

Sea Horse Duo 85

Daisies on Blue 89

Egret Bay 92

Squares in Squares 95

Sea Treasures 96

The Master Bedroom

Cosmetics Caddy 103

White Roses on Amethyst 105

Leafy Glade 106

Stack-n-Stitch Jewel Tone 108

Floral Surprise 111

Gold Ribbon 115

Country Star Quilt 117

Red Toile 120

The Kids' Room

Heart Swirls 124

My Favorite Pair of Jeans 126

Just Ducky 130

Happy Faces 133

Goldfish Bowl 134

Baby's Garden 136

Skateboard Pup 139

Tutu Bear 141

Pretty in Pink Kitty 144

The Christmas Collection

Noel 149

Christmas Sophistication 153

Fantasy Tree 154

Holiday Wonderland 156

Poinsettia Patchwork 158

Pink Poinsettia Elegance 160

Christmas Holly 162

The Gift 164

Santa's Workshop 166

Believe 169

General Information

Special Thanks 173

Buyer's Guide 173

Stitch Guide 174

The Kitchen

Often called "the heart of the home," the kitchen holds countless memories of bright sunny days and delicious sights and smells. In this chapter, you'll find plenty of cheerful projects that capture the sunshine, adding warmth and joy to your own family kitchen!

Checks & Cherries

Design by Kathy Wirth

With its cheerfully checked background and plump juicy cherries,
this terrific topper is a blossom of country comfort!

Skill Level: Beginner

Size: Fits high-count family-size tissue box

Materials

- 2 sheets stiff 7-count plastic canvas
- Coats & Clark Red Heart Classic worsted weight yarn Art. E267 as listed in color key
- Coats & Clark Red Heart Super Saver worsted weight yarn Art. E300 as listed in color key
- DMC 6-strand embroidery floss as listed in color key
- #16 tapestry needle
- #22 tapestry needle

Project Note

Use #16 tapestry needle with yarn and #22 tapestry needle with embroidery floss.

Instructions

1. Cut plastic canvas according to graphs (this page and page 8).

2. Stitch pieces following graphs, working uncoded areas with eggnog Continental Stitches; work white Smyrna Cross Stitches before the black ones.

3. When background stitching is completed, Backstitch stems with ultra dark pistachio green floss.

4. Using eggnog throughout, Overcast inside edges of top and bottom edges of sides and ends. Whipstitch sides to ends, then Whipstitch sides and ends to top. ❖

COLOR KEY	
Worsted Weight Yarn	**Yards**
☐ White #1	38
■ Black #12	45
▨ Paddy green #686	3
▨ Forest green #689	3
▨ Jockey red #902	4
▨ Country red #914	20
▨ Cardinal #917	6
Uncoded areas are eggnog #329 Continental Stitches	45
⁄ Eggnog #329 Overcasting and Whipstitching	
6-Strand Embroidery Floss	
⁄ Ultra dark pistachio green #890 Backstitch	4
Color numbers given are for Coats & Clark Red Heart Classic worsted weight yarn Art. E267 and Super Saver worsted weight yarn Art. E300 and DMC 6-strand embroidery floss.	

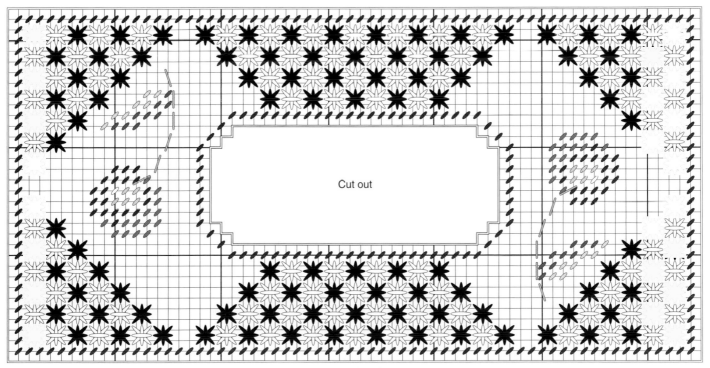

Checks & Cherries Top
65 holes x 33 holes
Cut 1

COLOR KEY

Worsted Weight Yarn	Yards
□ White #1	38
■ Black #12	45
▢ Paddy green #686	3
■ Forest green #689	3
▢ Jockey red #902	4
■ Country red #914	20
▢ Cardinal #917	6
Uncoded areas are eggnog #329 Continental Stitches	45

✎ Eggnog #329 Overcasting and Whipstitching

6-Strand Embroidery Floss

✎ Ultra dark pistachio green #890 Backstitch 4

Color numbers given are for Coats & Clark Red Heart Classic worsted weight yarn Art. E267 and Super Saver worsted weight yarn Art. E300 and DMC 6-strand embroidery floss.

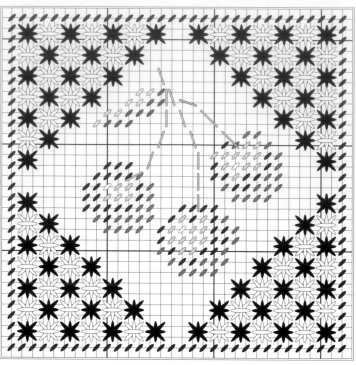

Checks & Cherries End
33 holes x 33 holes
Cut 2

Checks & Cherries Side
65 holes x 33 holes
Cut 2

To Market

Design by Janelle Giese

Full of lighthearted storybook charm, this little piggy doubles as a memo holder!

Skill Level: Advanced

Size: Fits boutique-style tissue box

Materials

- 1 1/2 sheets 7-count plastic canvas
- Coats & Clark Red Heart Classic worsted weight yarn Art. E267 as listed in color key
- 2-ply jute twine as listed in color key
- #3 pearl cotton as listed in color key
- #5 pearl cotton as listed in color key
- #16 tapestry needle
- 1 3/4-inch miniature clothespin

Project Note

The triangle, heart, square, inverted triangle and diamond shapes designate Continental Stitches.

Instructions

1. Cut plastic canvas according to graphs (pages 10 and 11).

2. Stitch pieces following graphs. Work Continental Stitches in uncoded areas as follows: shaded yellow areas with cornmeal, top with honey gold, shaded pink areas with light berry, and shaded blue areas with pale blue.

3. When background stitching is completed, use full strands yarn to work embroidery as follows: on front, new berry on basket cloth and country blue for shoulder strap; on right side, black at end of each chair arm; on back, light sage for leaves. Use 2 plies eggshell to work feather of pen on back.

4. Work all pearl cotton embroidery next, using #3 pearl cotton for lettering and parts of wagon, chair, desk and pig at desk as indicated.

5. Work #5 pearl cotton stitches following graphs, wrapping French Knots two times and working Straight Stitches on blue borders as follows: work first journey against direction of Continental Stitches, then second journey with direction of Continental Stitches.

6. Use full strand yarn to work the following embroidery: on right side, new berry for book cover; on back, warm brown for chair spindles.

7. Using jute twine through step 8, border center motifs with Backstitches where indicated. Attach clothespin where indicted, working around sides and through center opening of spring.

8. Overcast bottom edges of sides and opening on top. Whipstitch front and back to sides, making sure to put sides in correct places, then Whipstitch front, back and sides to top. ❖

COLOR KEY

Worsted Weight Yarn	Yards
◢ Black #12	2
▽ Eggshell #111	5
△ Cornmeal #220	10
♥ Tan #334	4
◢ Warm brown #336	7
▽ Nickel #401	1
♡ Light sage #631	5
◆ Dark sage #633	1
□ Honey gold #645	7
■ Seafoam #684	9
△ Pale rose #755	2
◢ Cameo rose #759	3
▼ New berry #760	9
◇ Light berry #761	8
◆ Windsor blue #808	22
∅ Country blue #882	2

Uncoded areas in shaded yellow areas
are cornmeal #220 Continental Stitches
Uncoded areas on top are honey
gold #645 Continental Stitches
Uncoded areas in shaded pink areas
are light berry #761 Continental Stitches
Uncoded areas in shaded blue areas
are pale blue #815 Continental Stitches   4

∕ Black #12 Straight Stitch	
∅ Eggshell #111 Backstitch and Straight Stitch	
∕ Warm brown #336 Straight Stitch	
∕ Light sage #631 Straight Stitch	
∕ New berry #760 Backstitch and Straight Stitch	
∅ Country blue #882 Straight Stitch	

Jute Twine

∕ Natural Backstitch, Overcasting and Whipstitching	16

#3 Pearl Cotton

∕ Black Backstitch and Straight Stitch	11

#5 Pearl Cotton

∕ Black Backstitch and Straight Stitch	21
● Black French Knot	
● Attach clothespin	

Color numbers given are for Coats & Clark Red Heart Classic
worsted weight yarn Art. E267.

To Market Top
30 holes x 30 holes
Cut 1

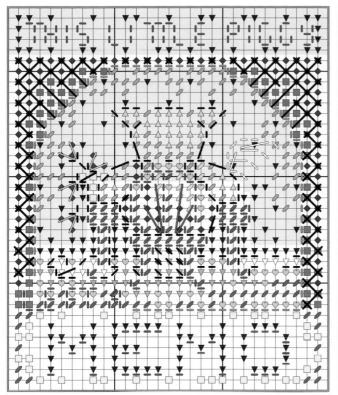

To Market Back
30 holes x 36 holes
Cut 1

To Market Front
30 holes x 36 holes
Cut 1

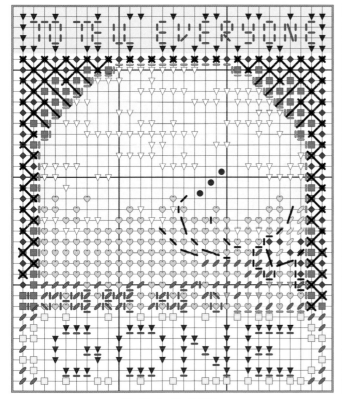

To Market Left Side
30 holes x 36 holes
Cut 1

To Market Right Side
30 holes x 36 holes
Cut 1

A Spot of Tea

Designs by Cynthia Roberts

Serve up some country charm with this warm and whimsical topper and coaster ensemble.

5. Cut ribbon into four 9-inch lengths. For each side, insert ribbon ends from back to front through holes indicated on graph; tie ribbon around handle of one coaster (see photo). ❖

COLOR KEY	
Worsted Weight Yarn	**Yards**
☐ Off-white	32
■ Dark red	26
☐ Light yellow	18
▨ Light green	16
Uncoded areas on coasters are light yellow Continental Stitches	
○ Light yellow French Knot	
● Attach ribbon	

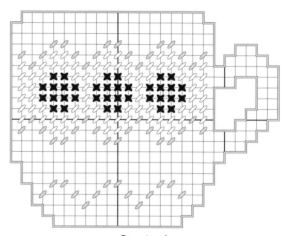

Coaster A
25 holes x 20 holes
Cut 2

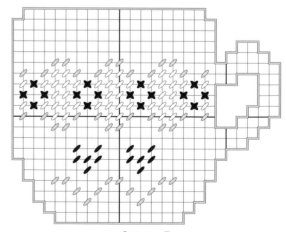

Coaster B
25 holes x 20 holes
Cut 2

Skill Level: Beginner

Size: Fits boutique-style tissue box

Materials

- 2 sheets 7-count plastic canvas
- Worsted weight yarn as listed in color key
- #16 tapestry needle
- 1 yard ¹/₈-inch-wide off-white satin ribbon
- Self-adhesive off-white felt

Instructions

1. Cut plastic canvas according to graphs (this page and page 14). Cut felt to fit cup part of coasters, leaving handles free.

2. Stitch and Overcast coasters following graphs, working uncoded areas with light yellow Continental Stitches. Attach felt to backside of each coaster.

3. Stitch sides and top following graphs.

4. Using light yellow throughout, Overcast inside edges of top and bottom edges of sides. Whipstitch sides together, then Whipstitch sides to top.

Graphs continued on page 14

Ruler of the Roost

Design by Kathy Wirth

When you're "hen-pecked" and hurried, one glance at this regal rooster will lift up your spirits with whimsical delight!

Skill Level: Beginner

Size: Fits boutique-style tissue box

Materials

- 1½ sheets stiff 7-count plastic canvas
- Coats & Clark Red Heart Classic worsted weight yarn Art. E267 as listed in color key
- Coats & Clark Red Heart Super Saver worsted weight yarn Art. E300 as listed in color key
- Coats & Clark Red Heart Kids worsted weight yarn Art. E711 as listed in color key
- #16 tapestry needle
- Hot-glue gun

Instructions

1. Cut plastic canvas according to graphs (this page and page 14).

2. Stitch and Overcast wings with yellow, then work black Cross Stitches, working over edges where indicated.

3. Stitch remaining pieces following graphs, working uncoded areas around roosters with linen Continental Stitches; uncoded wing area on each rooster will remain unstitched. Work yellow Cross Stitches and white stitches before filling in with black.

COLOR KEY	
Worsted Weight Yarn	**Yards**
☐ White #1	14
■ Black #12	25
☐ Linen #330	45
■ Country red #914	5
☐ Yellow #2230	17
Uncoded areas around roosters and on top are linen #330 Continental Stitches	
Color numbers given are for Coats & Clark Red Heart Classic worsted weight yarn Art. E267, Super Saver worsted weight yarn Art. E300 and Kids worsted weight yarn Art. E711.	

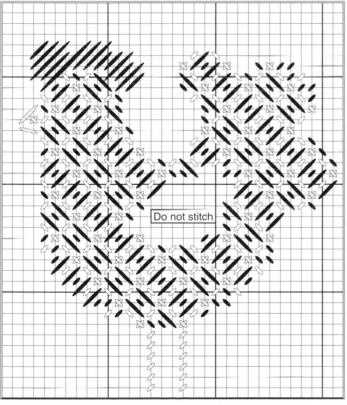

Ruler of the Roost Side
32 holes x 37 holes
Cut 4

Do not stitch

4. Using country red, Overcast opening on top and bottom edges of sides.

5. Using linen, Whip-stitch sides together, then Whipstitch sides to top.

6. Glue wings to sides in unstitched areas (see photo). ❖

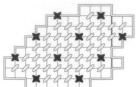

Wing
12 holes x 8 holes
Cut 4

COLOR KEY

Worsted Weight Yarn	Yards
☐ White #1	14
■ Black #12	25
☐ Linen #330	45
■ Country red #914	5
☐ Yellow #2230	17

Uncoded areas around roosters and on top are linen #330 Continental Stitches
Color numbers given are for Coats & Clark Red Heart Classic worsted weight yarn Art. E267, Super Saver worsted weight yarn Art. E300 and Kids worsted weight yarn Art. E711.

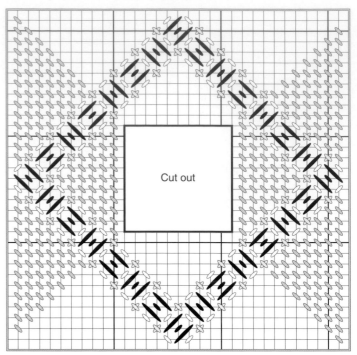

Ruler of the Roost Top
32 holes x 32 holes
Cut 1

A Spot of Tea

Continued from page 12

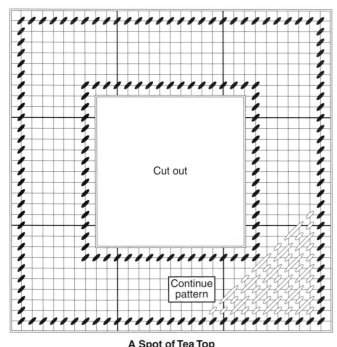

A Spot of Tea Top
30 holes x 30 holes
Cut 1

Cut out

Continue pattern

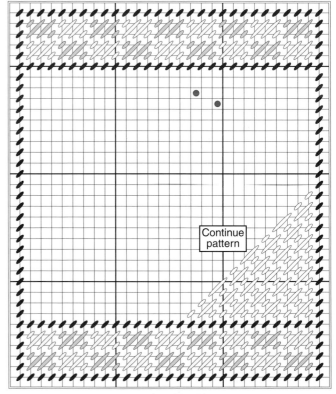

A Spot of Tea Side
30 holes x 36 holes
Cut 4

Continue pattern

Kitty Chef

Design by Janelle Giese

This culinary kitty helps out in the kitchen by cleverly keeping your spices in "check!"

Skill Level: Advanced

Size: Fits boutique-style tissue box

Materials
- 1½ sheets 7-count black plastic canvas
- ½ sheet clear 7-count black plastic canvas
- Uniek Needloft plastic canvas yarn as listed in color key
- #3 pearl cotton as listed in color key
- #16 tapestry needle
- Purchased salt and pepper shakers
- Thick white glue

Cutting & Stitching

1. Cut three topper side/back pieces, one topper top, one tray side and two tray bases from black plastic canvas; cut one topper front, two thumbs and two hands from clear plastic canvas according to graphs (pages 16, 25 and 26).

2. Following graphs throughout all stitching, stitch topper sides, back and top, working the variation on Hungarian Stitch following Fig. 1 (page 25) to produce gingham pattern.

3. Stitch topper front, working uncoded areas with white Continental Stitches and leaving blue highlighted Whipstitch lines and lavender joining area unworked at this time.

4. Using full strands yarn, Straight Stitch pupils on eyes with black, then Straight Stitch eye highlights with white. Use pearl cotton to work remaining embroidery, wrapping each French Knot one time for whisker dimples.

5. Stitch thumbs and hands, reversing one hand before stitching.

6. Place two tray base pieces together and stitch as one. Stitch

tray side, leaving overlap and shaded lavender areas unworked at this time.

7. Overcast opening on topper top and bottom edges of topper sides.

Assembly

1. Whipstitch sides to front following graph, using Continental Stitches at blue highlighted Whipstitch lines in colors indicated and using white where uncoded, but do not Whipstitch shaded lavender area at this time. Overcast extended edges of hat, fur points and shoulder where indicated.

2. Whipstitch back to sides. Whipstitch top to front, back and sides, using Continental Stitches at blue

highlighted Whipstitch line on front in colors indicated and using white where uncoded.

3. Overlap tray side where indicated, then match "X's" and lavender areas on tray sides and topper front. Complete the two rows of black Continental Stitches for tray side, working through all layers, Whipstitching tray side, topper front and topper side together while stitching.

4. Using red, Overcast top edge of tray side, continuing with Continental Stitches to Whipstitch top edge of tray side to topper front.

5. Whipstitch tray base in place with black, matching bracketed areas and working through all thicknesses.

6. Whipstitch bottom edge of one thumb to top edge of one hand between blue dots; Overcast

remaining edges. Repeat with remaining thumb and hand. Work black pearl cotton Straight Stitch on each hand.

7. Glue one hand to each side of tray, bending thumbs over top edge (see photo). Place tissue box inside topper and salt and pepper shakers in tray. ❖

COLOR KEY	
Plastic Canvas Yarn	**Yards**
■ Black #00	21
■ Red #01	25
■ Burgundy #03	14
▢ Baby yellow #21	1
▢ Silver #37	8
▢ Gray #38	2
▢ Beige #40	1
▢ White #41	29
■ Camel #43	1
Uncoded areas on front are white #41 Continental Stitches	
╱ Black #00 Straight Stitch	
╱ White #41 Straight Stitch	
#3 Pearl Cotton	
╱ Black Backstitch and Straight Stitch	3
● Black French Knot	
Color numbers given are for Uniek Needloft plastic canvas yarn.	

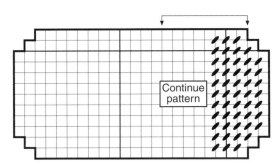

Kitty Chef Tray Base
24 holes x 12 holes
Cut 2 from black

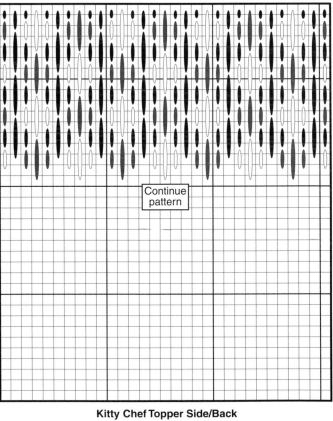

Kitty Chef Topper Side/Back
31 holes x 37 holes
Cut 3 from black

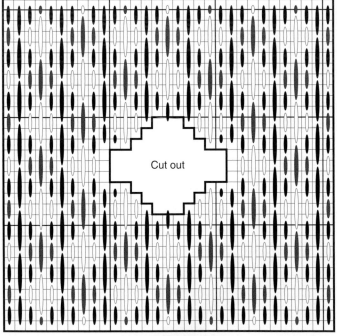

Kitty Chef Topper Top
31 holes x 31 holes
Cut 1 from black

Graphs continued on page 25

Apple Delight

Design by Angie Arickx

Sweet and fresh as a country morning, this fruit-laden topper is sure to perk up your spirits!

Skill Level: Beginner

Size: Fits regular-size tissue box

Materials

- 1½ sheets 7-count plastic canvas
- Uniek Needloft plastic canvas yarn as listed in color key
- #16 tapestry needle

Instructions

1. Cut plastic canvas according to graphs (this page and pages 18 and 19).

2. Stitch pieces following graphs, working uncoded areas with white Continental Stitches.

3. Using white throughout, Overcast inside edges of top, and bottom edges of sides and ends. Whipstitch sides to ends, then Whipstitch sides and ends to top. ❖

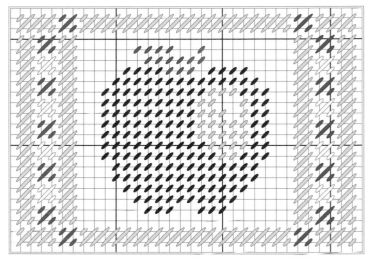

Apple Delight End
33 holes x 23 holes
Cut 2

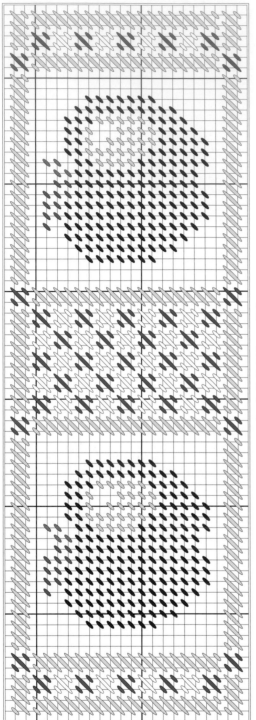

Apple Delight Long Side
67 holes x 23 holes
Cut 2

COLOR KEY	
Plastic Canvas Yarn	**Yards**
■ Red #01	23
▢ Christmas red #02	4
▨ Cinnamon #14	1
▨ Fern #23	34
▨ Holly #27	14
▢ White #41	42
Uncoded areas are white	
#41 Continental Stitches	
Color numbers given are for Uniek Needloft	
plastic canvas yarn.	

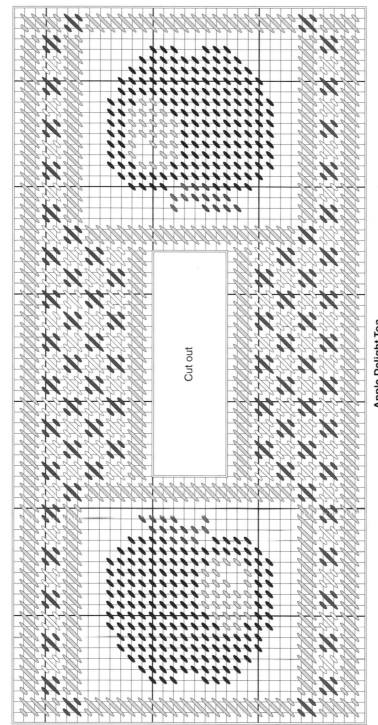

Apple Delight Top
67 holes x 33 holes
Cut 1

Cut out

Garden Bees

Design by Janelle Giese

These busy bees will keep you buzzing with springtime cheer
as they help you keep track of tiny treasures!

Skill Level: Advanced

Size: Fits boutique-style tissue box

Materials

- 4 sheets almond 7-count plastic canvas
- Uniek Needloft plastic canvas yarn as listed in color key
- DMC #3 pearl cotton as listed in color key
- DMC #5 pearl cotton as listed in color key
- DMC 6-strand embroidery floss as listed in color key
- #16 tapestry needle
- 3 (⅞-inch) brass cup hooks
- Thick white glue

Project Note

The triangle, heart, square, inverted triangle and diamond shapes designate Continental Stitches.

Cutting

1. Cut two fronts, four sides, two backs and one lid top from plastic canvas according to graphs (pages 21, 27 and 28).

2. Cut two 31-hole × 31-hole pieces for base, four 29-hole × 6-hole pieces for lid sides and three 5-hole × 5-hole pieces for hook supports. Base and lid side pieces will remain unstitched.

Front

1. Place the two front pieces together and stitch as one, working background with Continental Stitches and uncoded areas with eggshell Continental Stitches. Leave areas highlighted with pale yellow and blue highlighted line unworked at this time.

2. When background stitching is completed, work Straight Stitches for bees' wings with 1 ply white yarn. Complete wings by wrapping Backstitches around each wing with ultra dark beaver gray #5 pearl cotton (not graphed).

3. Work dark yellow beige Backstitches and Straight Stitches; work ultra dark beaver gray Backstitches and Straight Stitches next, passing over body of bees three times and door of bee hive six times.

4. Using 1 strand each of medium forest green and very dark forest green, work vines where indicated, couching with 2 plies very dark forest green embroidery floss.

5. Backstitch remaining leaves with very dark forest green and with medium forest green where indicated.

6. Stitch flowers next, working French Knots last as follows: for medium terra cotta, very dark garnet and dark yellow beige knots, wrap two times; for hyacinths, use a combination of 1 strand each navy blue and light violet, wrapping knot one time.

7. Overcast top edge with beige.

Sides, Back & Lid Top

1. Stitch lid top using variation on the Hungarian Stitch (page 25), working beige and white stitches first, then lemon stitches last. Do not stitch blue

highlighted lines at this time. Overcast inside edges with beige.

2. Continental Stitch and Overcast hook supports with white.

3. Place two back pieces together and stitch as one, leaving center area unworked as indicated.

4. Overcast inside edges with white. Using beige, Overcast around top edges from arrow to arrow and around bottom edges from arrow to arrow.

5. Place two side pieces together; stitch as one, working the variation on Hungarian Stitch as in step 1 and leaving blue highlighted line and areas highlighted with yellow unworked at this time. Repeat for remaining side, reversing before stitching.

6. Using beige, Overcast top edge; Overcast

Garden Bees Front
31 holes x 39 holes
Cut 2

COLOR KEY	
Plastic Canvas Yarn	**Yards**
Lemon #20	34
▽ Baby yellow #21	11
◇ Moss #25	3
■ Holly #27	2
Baby blue #36	2
♥ Silver #37	5
△ Gray #38	2
Beige #40	31
○ White #41	16
Uncoded areas on front are eggshell #39 Continental Stitches	6
White #41 Straight Stitch	
#3 Pearl Cotton	
✔ Navy blue #336 Straight Stitch	2
✔ Very dark forest green #986 Backstitch and Straight Stitch	3
✔ Medium forest green #988 Backstitch and Straight Stitch	2
✔ Very dark forest green #986 and medium forest green #988 Couching Stitch	
Dark yellow beige #3045 Backstitch and Straight Stitch	3
ᗡ Very dark garnet #902 Lazy Daisy Stitch	2
● Navy blue #336 and light violet #554 French Knot	1
● Medium terra cotta #356 French Knot	2
● Very dark garnet #902 French Knot	
○ Dark yellow beige #3045 French Knot	
#5 Pearl Cotton	
✔ Very dark beaver gray #844 Backstitch and Straight Stitch	5
6-Strand Embroidery Floss	
✔ Very dark forest green #986 Couching Stitch	1
● Attach cup hook	
Color numbers given are for Uniek Needloft plastic canvas yarn and DMC #3 and #5 pearl cotton and 6-strand embroidery floss.	

bottom edges from arrow to arrow, leaving blue highlighted line unworked at this time.

Assembly

1. Using beige, Whipstitch front piece to front edge of sides, then Whipstitch sides to back between arrows.

2. Place base pieces together and slide down to blue highlighted lines. Whipstitch to front with stitches shown on graph and Overcasting bottom edges while working beige stitches.

3. Whipstitch base to sides, working remaining rows of pattern stitch and beige stitches along blue highlighted line as indicated.

4. Using lemon, Whipstitch base to back along blue highlighted line.

5. Place one hook support on back where indicated with red lines. Screw cup hook into hook support and back; glue between pieces. Repeat with remaining hook supports and cup hooks.

6. Using beige throughout, Whipstitch short ends of lid sides together; then Overcast bottom edges. Place lid sides against wrong side of top at blue highlighted lines; Whipstitch to top with lemon Continental Stitches. Overcast outside edges of top with beige. ❖

Graphs continued on page 27

Sunflower Gingham

Designs by Kimberly A. Suber

*Bright as a golden meadow and warm as the summer sky,
this lovely tissue topper is like a breath of fresh air!*

flower center following graphs, working French Knots on flower center with full strand brown.

4. When background stitching is completed, work French Knots on ladybug with 2 plies black.

5. Stitch sides and top following graphs. Overcast inside edges of top with white.

6. Using medium blue throughout, Overcast bottom edges of sides. Whipstitch sides together, then Whipstitch sides to top.

7. Using photo as a guide, center and glue flowers and leaves to one side, placing leaves between flower petals. Glue flower center and ladybug to sunflower. ❖

Ladybug
4 holes x 5 holes
Cut 1

COLOR KEY	
Worsted Weight Yarn	**Yards**
☐ Light blue	48
☐ White	16
■ Medium blue	14
☐ Dark yellow	5
☐ Yellow	3
☐ Green	2
■ Red	1
■ Black	1
╱ Brown Overcasting	3
╱ Dark green Overcasting	2
● Brown French Knot	
● Black French Knot	

Skill Level: Beginner

Size: Fits boutique-style tissue box

Materials
- 1½ sheets 7-count plastic canvas
- 2 Uniek QuickShape plastic canvas hexagons
- Worsted weight yarn as listed in color key
- #16 tapestry needle
- Hot-glue gun

Project Note
Depending on actual size of boutique-style tissue box, this topper will be a very tight fit.

Instructions

1. Cut one sunflower from one plastic canvas hexagon and six leaves from remaining plastic canvas hexagon according to graphs (this page and page 25), cutting away gray areas.

2. Cut one flower center, one ladybug, one top and four sides from 7-count plastic canvas according to graphs (this page and page 24).

3. Stitch and Overcast flower, leaves, ladybug and

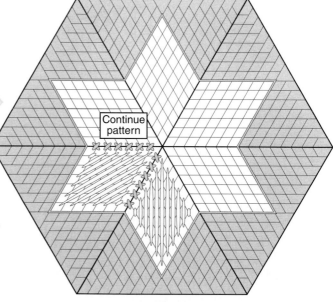

Sunflower
Cut 1 from 1 hexagon,
cutting away gray area

Graphs continued on page 24

Tropical Treat

Design by Kathleen Hurley

Friendly and fun, these prancing flamingos will put a smile in your heart!

Skill Level: Beginner

Size: Fits boutique-style tissue box

Materials
- 2 sheets black 7-count plastic canvas
- Coats & Clark Red Heart Classic worsted weight yarn Art. E267 as listed in color key
- #16 tapestry needle

Instructions

1. Cut plastic canvas according to graphs (this page and page 24).

2. Stitch pieces following graphs, leaving blue highlighted Whipstitch line on flamingo neck unworked at this time and filling in as needed with Slanted Gobelin Stitch pattern around plants and each flamingo.

3. When background stitching is completed, work French Knot eye on each flamingo with full strand yarn, wrapping one time.

4. Using grenadine and black, Overcast flamingo head and neck above top edges on sides.

COLOR KEY	
Worsted Weight Yarn	**Yards**
■ Black #12	62
■ Parakeet #513	6
■ Emerald green #676	8
■ Grenadine #730	16
■ Pink #737	16
╱ Pink #737 Straight Stitch	
● Black #12 French Knot	
Color numbers given are for Coats & Clark Red Heart Classic worsted weight yarn Art. E267.	

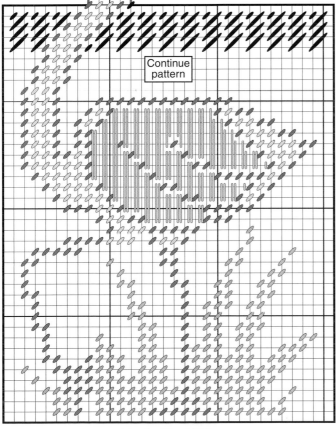

Tropical Treat Side
31 holes x 51 holes
Cut 4

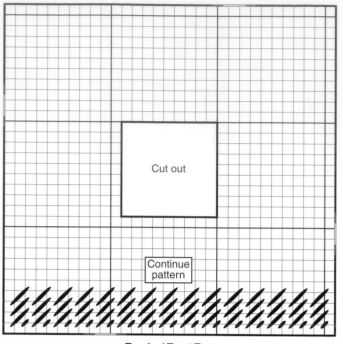

Tropical Treat Top
31 holes x 31 holes
Cut 1

5. Using black, Overcast inside edges of top and bottom edges of sides; Whipstitch sides together. Whipstitch sides to top with black, using grenadine and pink Continental Stitches where indicated along blue highlighted line. ❖

COLOR KEY	
Worsted Weight Yarn	**Yards**
■ Black #12	62
■ Parakeet #513	6
■ Emerald green #676	8
■ Grenadine #730	16
☐ Pink #737	16
╱ Pink #737 Straight Stitch	
● Black #12 French Knot	
Color numbers given are for Coats & Clark Red Heart Classic worsted weight yarn Art. E267.	

Sunflower Gingham
Continued from page 22

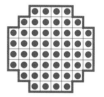

Sunflower Center
8 holes x 8 holes
Cut 1

COLOR KEY	
Worsted Weight Yarn	**Yards**
■ Light blue	48
☐ White	16
■ Medium blue	14
■ Dark yellow	5
☐ Yellow	3
■ Green	2
■ Red	1
■ Black	1
╱ Brown Overcasting	3
╱ Dark green Overcasting	2
● Brown French Knot	
● Black French Knot	

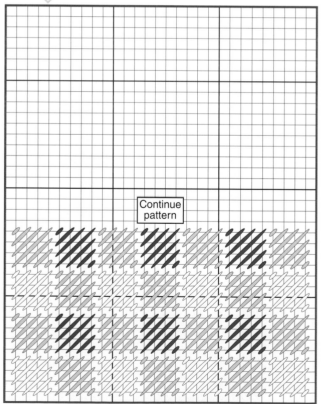

Sunflower Gingham Side
29 holes x 37 holes
Cut 4

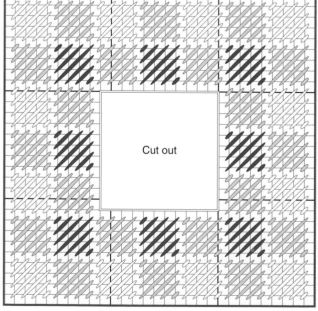

Sunflower Gingham Top
29 holes x 29 holes
Cut 1

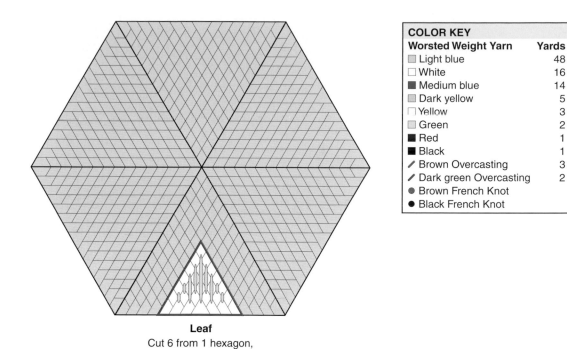

COLOR KEY	
Worsted Weight Yarn	**Yards**
☐ Light blue	48
☐ White	16
■ Medium blue	14
☐ Dark yellow	5
☐ Yellow	3
☐ Green	2
■ Red	1
■ Black	1
✎ Brown Overcasting	3
✎ Dark green Overcasting	2
● Brown French Knot	
● Black French Knot	

Leaf
Cut 6 from 1 hexagon,
cutting away gray area

Kitty Chef
Continued from page 16

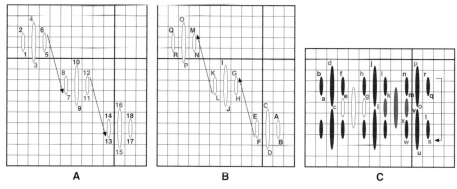

Fig. 1
Hungarian Stitch Variation

Following graph A, begin by working rows of lightest and rows of
darkest shades first. Work each row of color diagonally,
beginning at upper left corner and moving toward lower right
corner. Work each stitch from bottom to top (1 to 2, 3 to 4, etc.).

Following graph B, return by stitching diagonal row from
lower right to upper left, working each stitch
from top to bottom (A to B, C to D, etc.).

Following graph C, complete piece by working rows of the medium
shade last. Work each row horizontally, beginning at top of piece.
Work each stitch from bottom to top (a to b, c to d, etc.).

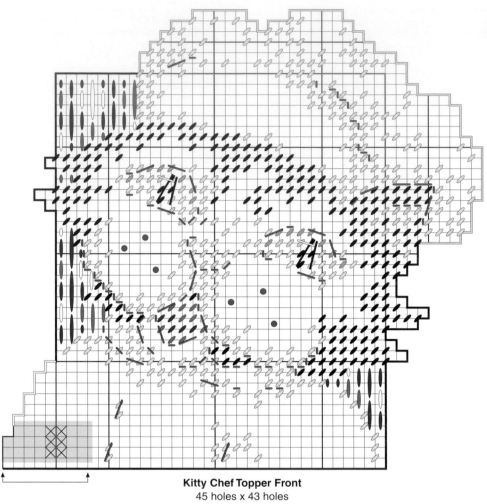

Kitty Chef Topper Front
45 holes x 43 holes
Cut 1 from clear

Kitty Chef Tray Side
70 holes x 3 holes
Cut 1 from black

COLOR KEY	
Plastic Canvas Yarn	**Yards**
■ Black #00	21
■ Red #01	25
■ Burgundy #03	14
☐ Baby yellow #21	1
☐ Silver #37	8
☐ Gray #38	2
☐ Beige #40	1
☐ White #41	29
☐ Camel #43	1
Uncoded areas on front are white #41 Continental Stitches	
✔ Black #00 Straight Stitch	
⁄ White #41 Straight Stitch	
#3 Pearl Cotton	
✔ Black Backstitch and Straight Stitch	3
● Black French Knot	
Color numbers given are for Uniek Needloft plastic canvas yarn.	

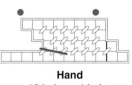

Hand
12 holes x 4 holes
Cut 2, reverse 1, from clear

Thumb
7 holes x 2 holes
Cut 2 from clear

Garden Bees
Continued from page 21

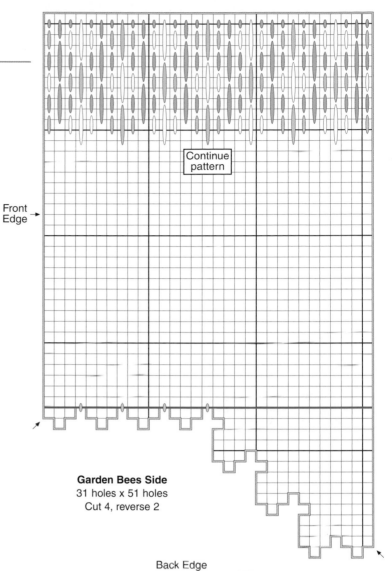

Garden Bees Side
31 holes x 51 holes
Cut 4, reverse 2

COLOR KEY	
Plastic Canvas Yarn	**Yards**
⬦ Lemon #20	34
▽ Baby yellow #21	11
◇ Moss #25	3
■ Holly #27	2
⬦ Baby blue #36	2
♥ Silver #37	5
△ Gray #38	2
⬦ Beige #40	31
⬦ White #41	16
Uncoded areas on front are eggshell #39 Continental Stitches	6
⬦ White #41 Straight Stitch	
#3 Pearl Cotton	
╱ Navy blue #336 Straight Stitch	2
╱ Very dark forest green #986 Backstitch and Straight Stitch	3
╱ Medium forest green #988 Backstitch and Straight Stitch	2
╱ Very dark forest green #986 and medium forest green #988 Couching Stitch	
╱ Dark yellow beige #3045 Backstitch and Straight Stitch	3
⌁ Very dark garnet #902 Lazy Daisy Stitch	2
● Navy blue #336 and light violet #554 French Knot	1
○ Medium terra cotta #356 French Knot	2
● Very dark garnet #902 French Knot	
○ Dark yellow beige #3045 French Knot	
#5 Pearl Cotton	
╱ Very dark beaver gray #844 Backstitch and Straight Stitch	5
6-Strand Embroidery Floss	
╱ Very dark forest green #986 Couching Stitch	1
● Attach cup hook	

Color numbers given are for Uniek Needloft plastic canvas yarn and DMC #3 and #5 pearl cotton and 6-strand embroidery floss.

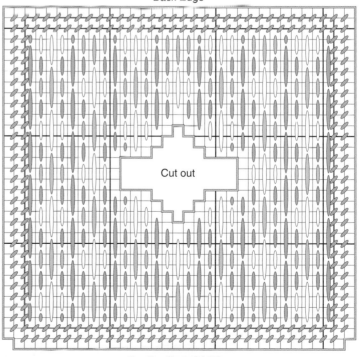

Garden Bees Lid Top
33 holes x 32 holes
Cut 1

COLOR KEY

Plastic Canvas Yarn	Yards
⬭ Lemon #20	34
▽ Baby yellow #21	11
◇ Moss #25	3
■ Holly #27	2
⬭ Baby blue #36	2
♥ Silver #37	5
△ Gray #38	2
⬭ Beige #40	31
⬭ White #41	16
Uncoded areas on front are eggshell #39 Continental Stitches	6
⬭ White #41 Straight Stitch	

#3 Pearl Cotton

╱ Navy blue #336 Straight Stitch	2
╱ Very dark forest green #986 Backstitch and Straight Stitch	3
╱ Medium forest green #988 Backstitch and Straight Stitch	2
╱ Very dark forest green #986 and medium forest green #988 Couching Stitch	
╱ Dark yellow beige #3045 Backstitch and Straight Stitch	3
ⅅ Very dark garnet #902 Lazy Daisy Stitch	2
● Navy blue #336 and light violet #554 French Knot	1
◐ Medium terra cotta #356 French Knot	2
● Very dark garnet #902 French Knot	
○ Dark yellow beige #3045 French Knot	

#5 Pearl Cotton

╱ Very dark beaver gray #844 Backstitch and Straight Stitch	5

6-Strand Embroidery Floss

╱ Very dark forest green #986 Couching Stitch	1
● Attach cup hook	

Color numbers given are for Uniek Needloft plastic canvas yarn and DMC #3 and #5 pearl cotton and 6-strand embroidery floss.

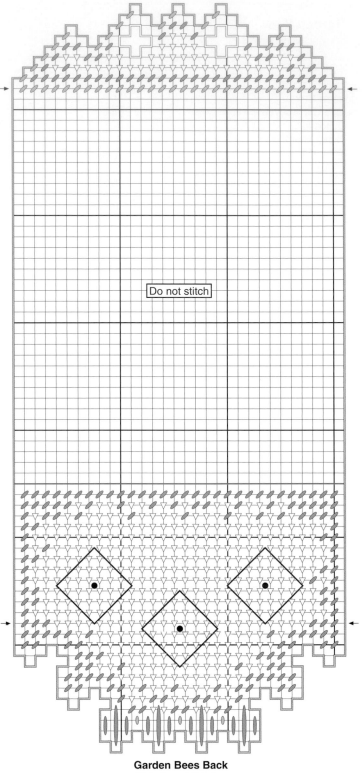

Do not stitch

Garden Bees Back
31 holes x 70 holes
Cut 2

The Family Room

From after-school play dates to family reunions,
this popular room is frequently the center of family life.
In this chapter we offer a vivid variety of fabulous
projects to meet any occasion in spectacular style!

Tribal Motif

Design by Kristine Loffredo

*The primitive symbols and primordial power of this tribal topper
will soon have you marching to the beat of an ancient drum!*

Skill Level: Beginner

Size: Fits boutique-style tissue box

Materials

- 2 sheets stiff 7-count plastic canvas
- Uniek Needloft plastic canvas yarn as listed in color key
- Lightweight jute as listed in color key
- #16 tapestry needle

Instructions

1. Cut plastic canvas according to graphs.

2. Stitch pieces following graphs, working fern Back-stitches when background stitching is completed.

3. Using brown throughout, Overcast inside edges of top and bottom edges of sides. Whipstitch sides together, then Whipstitch sides to top. ❖

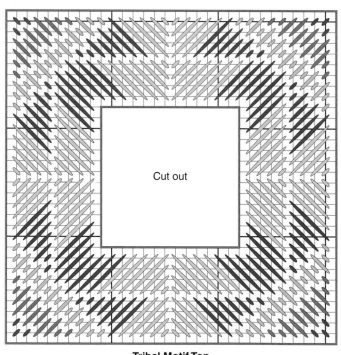

Tribal Motif Top
31 holes x 31 holes
Cut 1

Tribal Motif Side
31 holes x 37 holes
Cut 4

Pastel Patchwork

Design by Alida Macor

Pinstriped and perfect, this quilt-inspired confection adds pastel panache to your favorite room!

Skill Level: Beginner

Size: Fits boutique-style tissue box

Materials
- 1½ sheets 7-count plastic canvas
- Darice Nylon Plus plastic canvas yarn as listed in color key
- #16 tapestry needle

Instructions

1. Cut and stitch plastic canvas according to graphs.

2. Overcast inside edges of top with white. Using sail blue, Overcast bottom edges of sides; Whipstitch sides together, then Whipstitch sides to top. ❖

COLOR KEY	
Plastic Canvas Yarn	**Yards**
☐ White #01	23
■ Sail blue #04	41
☐ Baby blue #05	16
☐ Lemon #25	8
Color numbers given are for Darice Nylon Plus plastic canvas yarn.	

Pastel Patchwork Side
31 holes x 37 holes
Cut 4

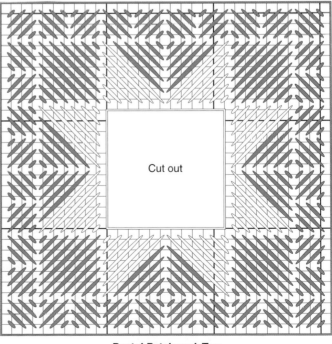

Pastel Patchwork Top
31 holes x 31 holes
Cut 1

Woven Lattice

Design by Kristine Loffredo

Intricate stitchwork and captivating color make this stately topper a true work of art!

Skill Level: Beginner

Size: Fits regular-size tissue box

Materials

- 2 sheets stiff 7-count plastic canvas
- Uniek Needloft plastic canvas yarn as listed in color key
- #16 tapestry needle

Instructions

1. Cut plastic canvas according to graphs (pages 33 and 34).

2. Stitch pieces following graphs, working beige Cross Stitches before working holly stitches over ends of Cross Stitches.

3. Using dark royal throughout, Overcast inside edges of top and bottom edges of sides and ends. Whipstitch sides to ends, then Whipstitch sides and ends to top. ❖

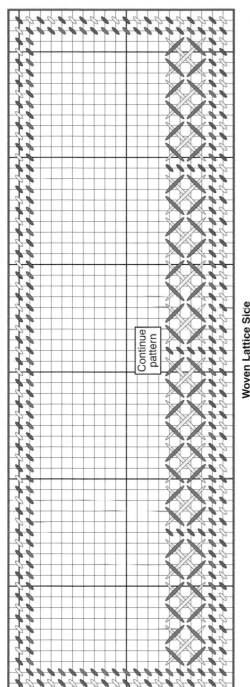

Woven Lattice Side
64 holes x 21 holes
Cut 2

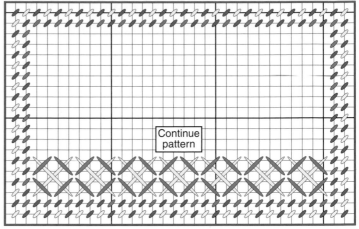

Woven Lattice End
33 holes x 21 holes
Cut 2

COLOR KEY	
Plastic Canvas Yarn	**Yards**
■ Holly #27	31
☐ Beige #40	41
■ Dark royal #48	26
Color numbers given are for Uniek Needloft plastic canvas yarn.	

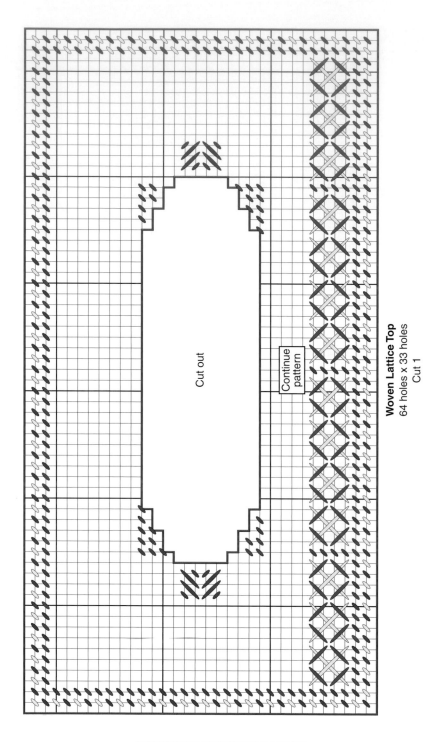

Woven Lattice Top
64 holes x 33 holes
Cut 1

Cut out

Continue pattern

COLOR KEY	
Plastic Canvas Yarn	**Yards**
■ Holly #27	31
□ Beige #40	41
■ Dark royal #48	26
Color numbers given are for Uniek Needloft plastic canvas yarn.	

God Bless This Home

Design by Kathy Wirth

Stitched in the primary colors of a crayon drawing, this
irresistible tissue topper glows with childlike appeal!

Skill Level: Beginner

Size: Fits boutique-style tissue box

Materials

- 1½ sheets 7-count plastic canvas
- Uniek Needloft plastic canvas yarn as listed in color key
- #3 pearl cotton as listed in color key
- #16 tapestry needle
- #20 tapestry needle

Project Note

Use #16 tapestry needle with yarn and #20 tapestry needle with pearl cotton.

Instructions

1. Cut plastic canvas according to graphs (page 37).

2. Stitch pieces following graphs, working uncoded areas with black Continental Stitches.

3. When background stitching is completed, embroider lettering on sides with white pearl cotton.

4. Overcast inside opening on top with bright blue yarn and bottom edges of sides with black yarn. Whipstitch sides together with black and white; Whipstitch sides to top with black. ❖

Graphs continued on page 37

Southwestern Quilt

Design by Kimberly A. Suber

*Jeweled mosaics and rustic crosses will brighten your home
with the majesty of the Southwestern sky!*

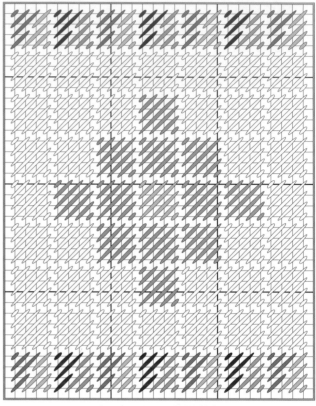

Southwestern Quilt Side
29 holes x 37 holes
Cut 4

Skill Level: Beginner

Size: Fits boutique-style tissue box

Materials
- 1¹/₂ sheets 7-count plastic canvas
- Uniek Needloft plastic canvas yarn as listed in color key
- #16 tapestry needle

Project Note
Depending on actual size of boutique-style tissue box, this topper will be a very tight fit.

Instructions
1. Cut and stitch plastic canvas according to graphs.

2. Using turquoise throughout, Overcast inside edges of top and bottom edges of sides. Whipstitch sides together, then Whipstitch sides to top. ❖

COLOR KEY	
Plastic Canvas Yarn	**Yards**
■ Burgundy #03	10
▨ Tangerine #11	11
☐ Eggshell #39	45
▨ Turquoise #54	30
■ Bright purple #64	10
Color numbers given are for Uniek Needloft plastic canvas yarn.	

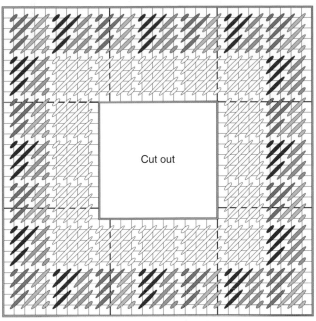

Southwestern Quilt Top
29 holes x 29 holes
Cut 1

COLOR KEY	
Plastic Canvas Yarn	**Yards**
■ Burgundy #03	10
■ Tangerine #11	11
□ Eggshell #39	45
■ Turquoise #54	30
■ Bright purple #64	10
Color numbers given are for Uniek Needloft plastic canvas yarn.	

COLOR KEY	
Plastic Canvas Yarn	**Yards**
■ Black #00	55
■ Christmas red #02	3
■ Tangerine #11	7
■ Fern #23	3
■ Royal #32	8
□ White #41	9
■ Bright blue #60	8
□ Bright yellow #63	3
■ Bright purple #64	9
Uncoded areas are black #00 Continental Stitches	
#3 Pearl Cotton	
╱ White Backstitch and Straight Stitch	13
Color numbers given are for Uniek Needloft plastic canvas yarn.	

God Bless This Home

Continued from page 35

God Bless This Home Top
32 holes x 32 holes
Cut 1

God Bless This Home Side
32 holes x 37 holes
Cut 4

End Table Organizer

Design by Angie Arickx

This handy organizer is as pretty as it is practical! You'll love its convenient charm!

Skill Level: Intermediate

Size: Fits regular-size tissue box

Materials

- 2 sheets 7-count plastic canvas
- Uniek Needloft plastic canvas yarn as listed in color key
- #16 tapestry needle

Instructions

1. Cut plastic canvas according to graphs (this page and pages 39 and 40).

2. Stitch pieces following graphs, working uncoded areas with white Continental Stitches, but leaving red highlighted Whipstitch lines on topper sides unworked.

3. Using white through step 5, Overcast top edges of pocket ends and sides, inside edges of top and bottom edges of topper ends.

4. Using photo as a guide, Whipstitch pocket ends to topper sides along red highlighted lines and to pocket sides, then Whipstitch pocket bottoms to pocket sides and ends and to topper sides.

5. Whipstitch topper sides to topper ends, then Whipstitch sides and ends to top. ❖

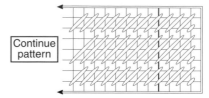

Continue pattern

Organizer Pocket Bottom
64 holes x 8 holes
Cut 2

COLOR KEY	
Plastic Canvas Yarn	**Yards**
☐ Moss #25	18
☐ White #41	151
☐ Lilac #45	10
Uncoded areas are white #41 Continental Stitches	
Color numbers given are for Uniek Needloft plastic canvas yarn.	

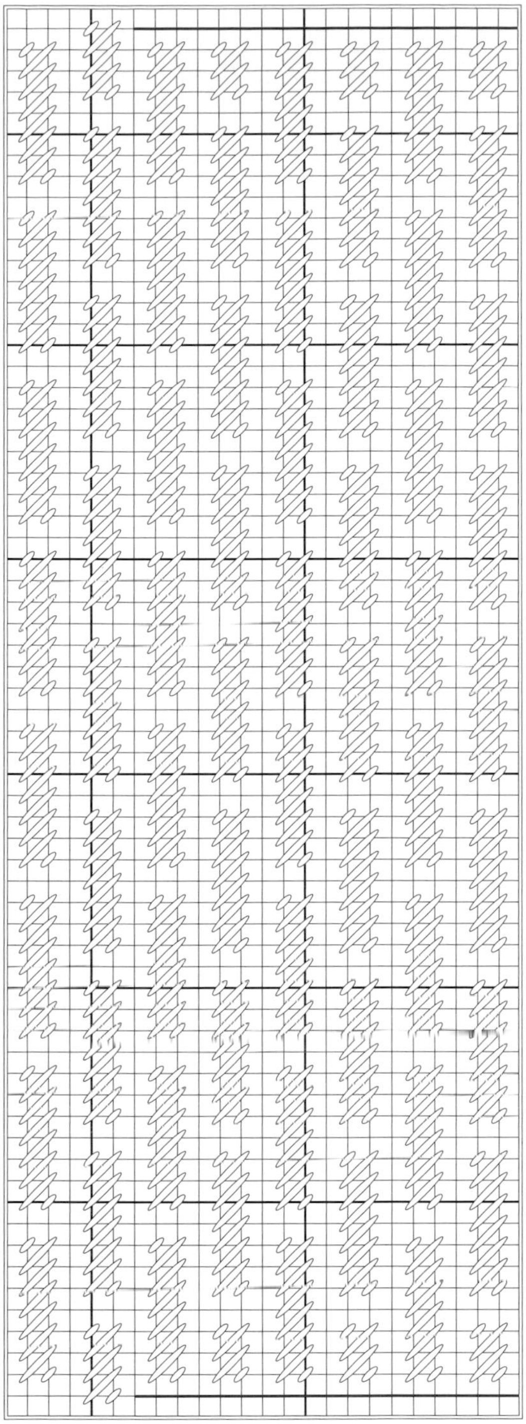

Organizer Topper Side
66 holes x 24 holes
Cut 2

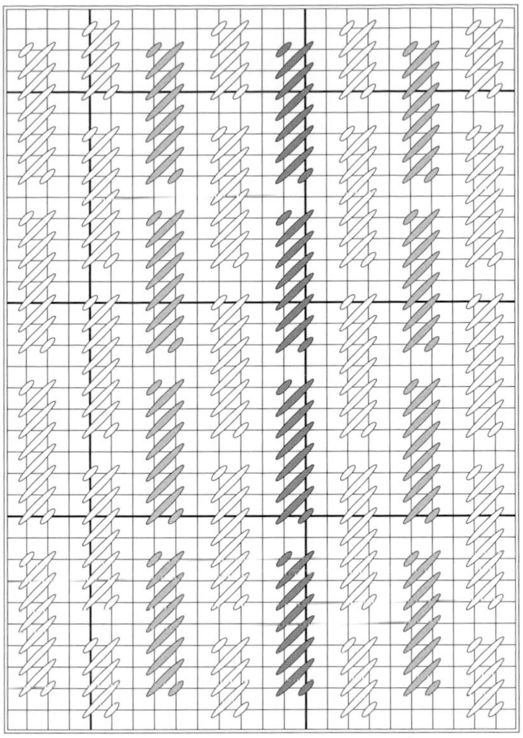

Organizer Topper End
34 holes x 24 holes
Cut 2

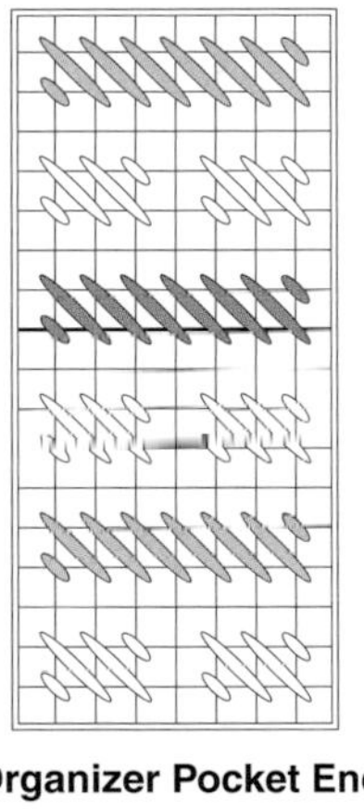

Organizer Pocket End
8 holes x 18 holes
Cut 4

COLOR KEY	
Plastic Canvas Yarn	**Yards**
Moss #25	18
White #41	151
Lilac #45	10
Uncoded areas are white	
#41 Continental Stitches	
Color numbers given are for Uniek Needloft plastic canvas yarn.	

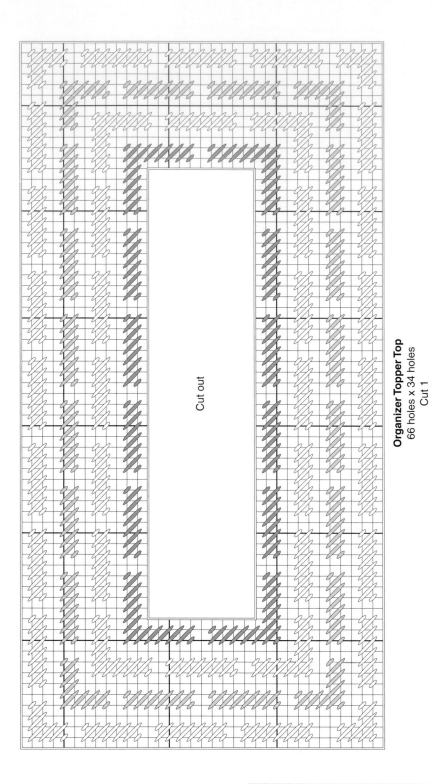

Organizer Topper Top
66 holes x 34 holes
Cut 1

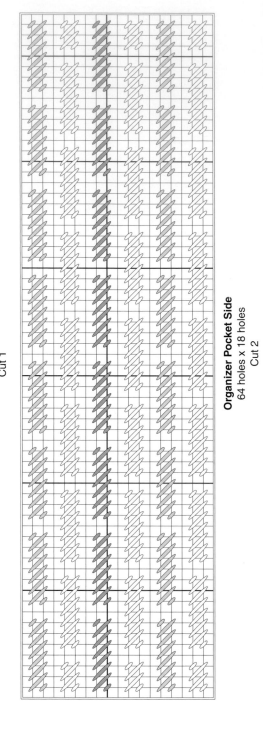

Organizer Pocket Side
64 holes x 18 holes
Cut 2

Cut out

COLOR KEY	
Plastic Canvas Yarn	**Yards**
☐ Moss #25	18
☐ White #41	151
☐ Lilac #45	10

Uncoded areas are white
#41 Continental Stitches
Color numbers given are for Uniek
Needloft plastic canvas yarn.

My Favorite Things

Design by Ronda Bryce

Personalize any room with this delightfully detailed showcase of some of life's tiny treasures!

Skill Level: Beginner

Size: Fits boutique-style tissue box

Materials

- 2 sheets clear 7-count plastic canvas
- 1 sheet black 7-count plastic canvas
- Uniek Needloft plastic canvas yarn as listed in color key
- Lion Chenille Sensations acrylic yarn from Lion Brand Yarn Co. as listed in color key
- #16 tapestry needle
- Sewing or needlework miniatures
- Small pewter cross charm
- 4 1/2 inches 1/4-inch-wide green satin ribbon
- 2 round green toothpicks
- 2 (5mm) silver beads
- Hand-sewing needle
- Green sewing thread
- Sewing thread as needed to match miniatures
- Plain white paper
- Craft glue

Topper

1. Cut front, back, sides and top from clear plastic canvas according to graphs (pages 42 and 43).

2. Stitch pieces following graphs. For fringe, cut 8-inch lengths in yarn colors and amounts as follows: 20 burgundy, 12 red, four holly, four dark royal, four lemon and two white.

3. Attach each 8-inch length where indicated with a Lark's Head Knot; trim to about 1 inch after all are attached.

4. Overcast inside edges on top with red plastic canvas yarn. Using brick chenille yarn, Overcast bottom edges of front, back and sides.

5. Using brick, Whipstitch front and back to sides, then Whipstitch sides to top. Whipstitch front and back to top with red and brick.

Basket

1. Cut sides, ends and handle from black plastic canvas according to graphs (page 43). Cut one 13-hole × 19-hole piece from black plastic canvas for basket bottom.

2. Stitch pieces following graphs. Basket bottom will remain unstitched.

3. Using brown, Whipstitch sides to ends, then Whipstitch sides and ends to unstitched bottom. Whipstitch handle ends to top edges of basket ends inside brackets. Do not stitch remaining edges.

4. For balls of yarn, cut about five yards each of lemon, burgundy, red, dark royal and holly. Roll each into a ball; tie off.

5. For knitting needles, glue a silver bead to one end of each toothpick; allow to dry thoroughly. Insert "needles" into a ball of yarn.

Bible

1. Cut two Bible covers and one spine from black plastic canvas according to graphs.

2. Stitch pieces following graphs, then Whip-stitch one cover to each side of spine; Overcast remaining edges.

3. For Bible pages, cut plain white paper into seven 2¼-inch x 1½-inch rectangles. Stack pages together. Fold pages in half so they measure 1⅛ inch x 1½ inch.

4. Place pages inside cover. Using black yarn, make a long stitch down spine over fold to hold pages in place.

5. For bookmark, thread end of green ribbon through cross charm; fold end over and tack down with hand-sewing needle and green thread. Trim other end to desired length. Tack book mark to Bible with green thread.

Assembly

1. Use photo as a guide throughout assembly. Using brown, tack basket to right front corner of topper, making sure bottom edges are even.

2. Place balls of yarn in basket, tacking in place if desired.

3. Tack Bible and miniatures to top, gluing for extra stability if desired. ❖

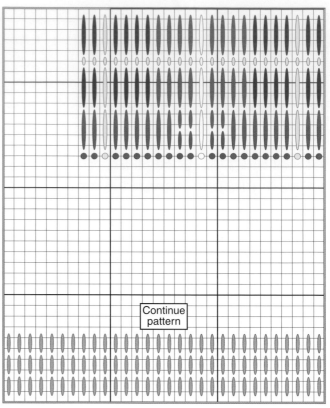

My Favorite Things Back
30 holes x 37 holes
Cut 1 from clear

Back Edge

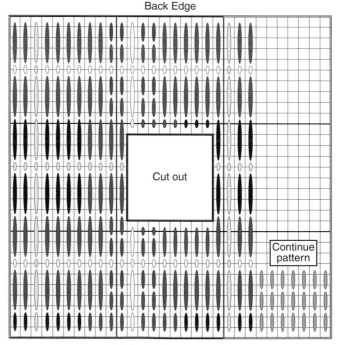

Cut out

Continue pattern

My Favorite Things Top
30 holes x 30 holes
Cut 1 from clear

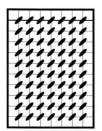

Bible Cover
8 holes x 11 holes
Cut 2 from black

Bible Spine
2 holes x 11 holes
Cut 1 from black

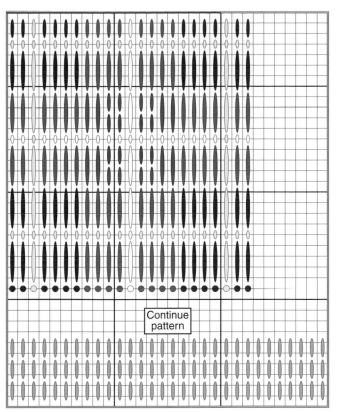

My Favorite Things Front
30 holes x 37 holes
Cut 1 from clear

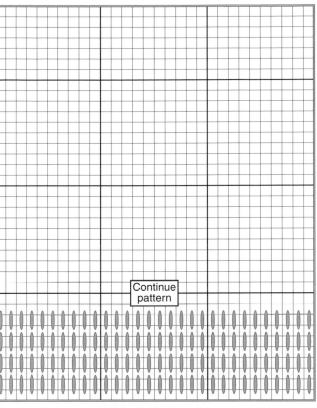

My Favorite Things Side
30 holes x 37 holes
Cut 2 from clear

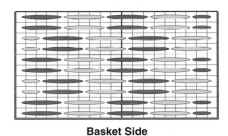

Basket Side
19 holes x 10 holes
Cut 2 from black

COLOR KEY	
Chenille Acrylic Yarn	**Yards**
■ Brick #134	45
Plastic Canvas Yarn	
■ Black #00	5
■ Red #01	21
■ Burgundy #03	21
■ Brown #15	9
□ Lemon #20	15
■ Holly #27	9
□ White #41	5
□ Camel #43	5
■ Dark royal #48	9
● Red #01 Lark's Head Knot	
● Burgundy #03 Lark's Head Knot	
○ Lemon #20 Lark's Head Knot	
● Holly #27 Lark's Head Knot	
○ White #41 Lark's Head Knot	
● Dark royal #48 Lark's Head Knot	

Color numbers given are for Lion Brand Yarn Co.
Lion Chenille Sensations acrylic yarn and Uniek
Needloft plastic canvas yarn.

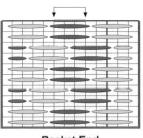

Basket End
13 holes x 10 holes
Cut 2 from black

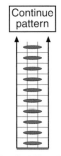

Basket Handle
3 holes x 44 holes
Cut 1 from black

Old Glory Quilt Block

Design by Angie Arickx

*Patriotic emblems unite with the antique beauty of quilts to give
this terrific tissue topper all the symbols of historic Americana!*

Skill Level: Beginner

Size: Fits regular-size tissue box

Materials

- 1½ sheets 7-count plastic canvas
- Uniek Needloft plastic canvas yarn as listed in color key
- #16 tapestry needle

Instructions

1. Cut plastic canvas according to graphs (pages 45 and 46).

2. Stitch pieces following graphs, working uncoded areas with dark royal Continental Stitches.

3. Work white French Knots when background stitching is completed.

4. Using dark royal throughout, Overcast inside edges of top and bottom edges of sides and ends. Whipstitch sides to ends, then Whipstitch sides and ends to top. ❖

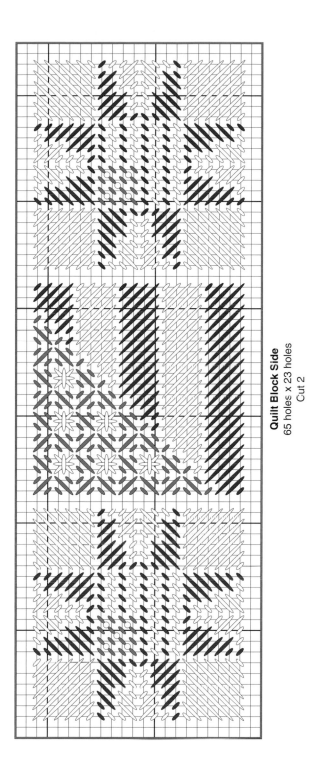

Quilt Block Side
65 holes x 23 holes
Cut 2

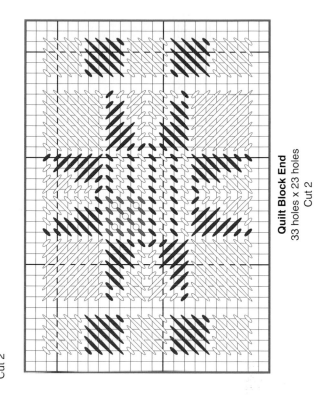

Quilt Block End
33 holes x 23 holes
Cut 2

COLOR KEY	
Plastic Canvas Yarn	**Yards**
■ Red #01	32
□ White #41	41
■ Dark royal #48	38
Uncoded areas are dark royal #48 Continental Stitches	
White #41 French Knot	
Color numbers given are for Uniek Needloft plastic canvas yarn.	

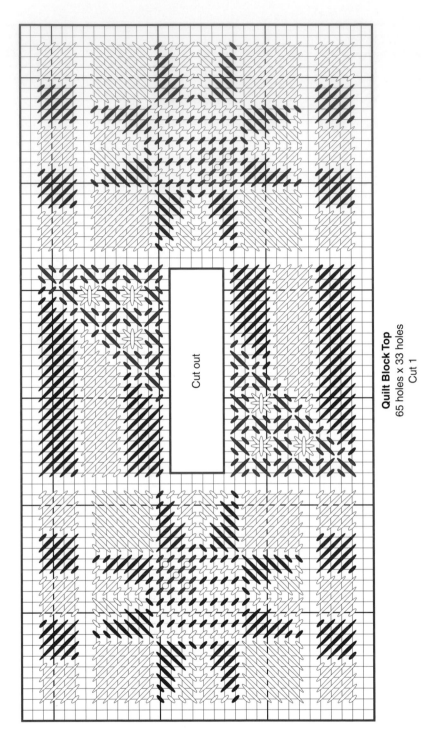

Quilt Block Top
65 holes x 33 holes
Cut 1

Cut out

COLOR KEY	
Plastic Canvas Yarn	**Yards**
■ Red #01	32
□ White #41	41
■ Dark royal #48	38
Uncoded areas are dark royal #48 Continental Stitches	
White #41 French Knot	
Color numbers given are for Uniek Needloft plastic canvas yarn.	

New Mexico

Design by Barbara Ivie

You'll love the desert warmth and artisan's appeal of this spectacular Southwestern topper!

Skill Level: Beginner

Size: Fits boutique-style tissue box

Materials

- 1¹/₂ sheets stiff 7-count plastic canvas
- Coats & Clark Red Heart Classic worsted weight yarn Art. E267 as listed in color key
- #16 tapestry needle

Instructions

1. Cut and stitch plastic canvas according to graphs (page 50).

2. Using black throughout, Overcast inside edges of top and bottom edges of sides. Whipstitch sides together; then Whipstitch sides to top. ❖

Graphs continued on page 50

Missing Pieces

Design by Ronda Bryce

This fascinating topper is so clever and unique that it makes a wonderful conversation "piece!"

Skill Level: Beginner

Size: Fits boutique-style tissue box

Materials

- 2 sheets black 7-count plastic canvas
- Uniek Needloft plastic canvas yarn as listed in color key
- #16 tapestry needle
- 4 (3-inch) squares black felt
- Hand-sewing needle
- Black sewing thread

Instructions

1. Cut plastic canvas according to graphs (pages 49 and 50).

2. Stitch and Overcast missing pieces following graphs, working one missing side piece with red as graphed, one with royal, one with lilac and one with purple.

3. Stitch topper pieces following graphs, working uncoded areas with burgundy Continental Stitches.

4. Using black, Overcast inside edges of top and sides and bottom edges of sides.

5. With hand-sewing needle and black thread, Whipstitch a piece of felt to back of each side, covering opening.

6. Using black, Whipstitch sides together, then Whipstitch sides to top.

7. Using black yarn, tack three missing pieces to top and two to sides (see photo). ❖

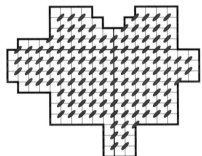

Missing Side Piece
18 holes x 14 holes
Cut 4
Stitch 1 as graphed,
1 with royal,
1 with lilac
and 1 with purple

COLOR KEY	
Plastic Canvas Yarn	**Yards**
■ Black #00	29
■ Red #02	11
☐ Lavender #05	13
☐ Gold #17	10
■ Royal #32	14
☐ Sail blue #35	14
☐ Lilac #45	12
■ Purple #46	14
☐ Mermaid #53	10
Uncoded areas are burgundy	
#03 Continental Stitches	11
Color numbers given are for Uniek Needloft plastic canvas yarn.	

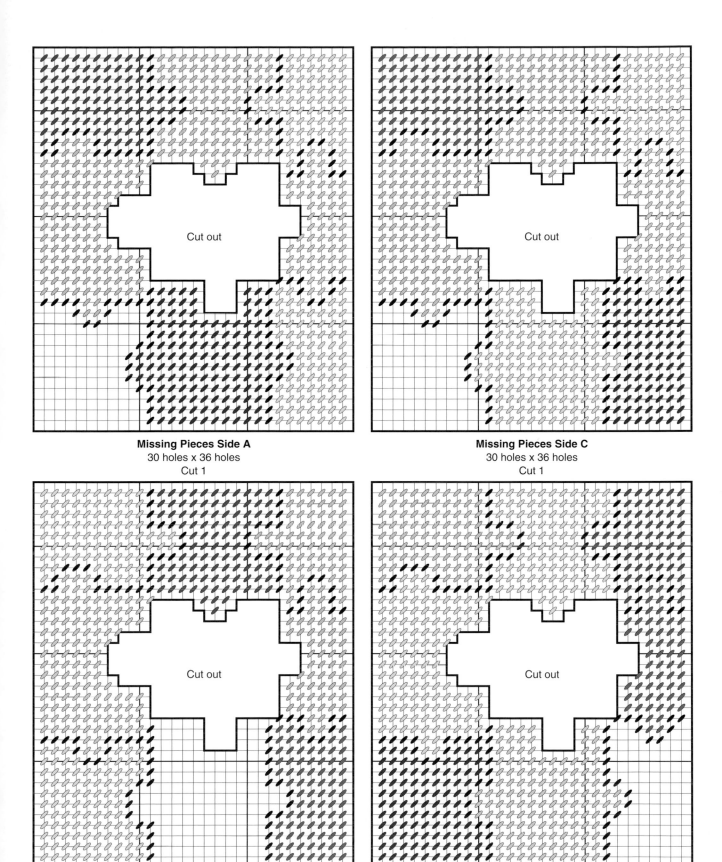

Missing Pieces Side A
30 holes x 36 holes
Cut 1

Missing Pieces Side C
30 holes x 36 holes
Cut 1

Missing Pieces Side B
30 holes x 36 holes
Cut 1

Missing Pieces Side D
30 holes x 36 holes
Cut 1

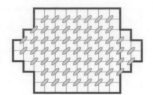

Missing Top Piece
12 holds x 8 holes
Cut 1

COLOR KEY	
Plastic Canvas Yarn	**Yards**
■ Black #00	29
■ Red #02	11
▨ Lavender #05	13
☐ Gold #17	10
■ Royal #32	14
☐ Sail blue #35	14
▨ Lilac #45	12
■ Purple #46	14
☐ Mermaid #53	10
Uncoded areas are burgundy	
#03 Continental Stitches	11
Color numbers given are for Uniek Needloft plastic canvas yarn.	

Missing Pieces Top
30 holes x 30 holes
Cut 1

New Mexico
Continued from page 47

COLOR KEY	
Worsted Weight Yarn	**Yards**
☐ Off white #3	21
■ Black #12	34
■ Teal #48	13
■ Bronze #286	10
☐ Peacock green #508	11
Color numbers given are for Coats & Clark Red Heart Classic worsted weight yarn Art. E267.	

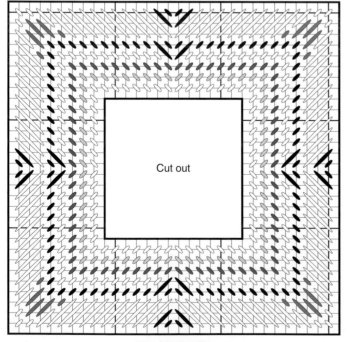

New Mexico Top
31 holes x 31 holes
Cut 1

New Mexico Side
31 holes x 37 holes
Cut 4

The Living Room

Living rooms often range from warm family retreats, full of easy-chair comfort, to stunning showplaces for fine antiques. In this chapter you'll find plenty of decorator accents perfectly suited for any style along the spectrum!

Victorian Elegance

Design by Kathy Barwick

Intricately detailed and pastel-pretty, this delectable topper will fill your home with stately charm!

Skill Level: Beginner

Size: Fits boutique-style tissue box

Materials

- 1½ sheets 7-count plastic canvas
- Worsted weight yarn as listed in color key
- ⅛-inch-wide wire-edge ribbon as listed in color key
- #16 tapestry needle

COLOR KEY	
Worsted Weight Yarn	**Yards**
▨ Rose	92
▨ Baby green	92
▨ Mint green	92
▢ Off-white	92
⅛-Inch Wire-Edge Ribbon	
⁄ Metallic gold Overcasting and Whipstitching	7

Instructions

1. Cut plastic canvas according to graphs.

2. Stitch pieces following graphs, working large rose Cross Stitches before working off-white Upright Cross Stitches over center of rose Cross Stitches.

3. Overcast inside edges of top and bottom edges of sides with gold ribbon. Whipstitch sides together with mint green, then Whipstitch sides to top with gold ribbon. ❖

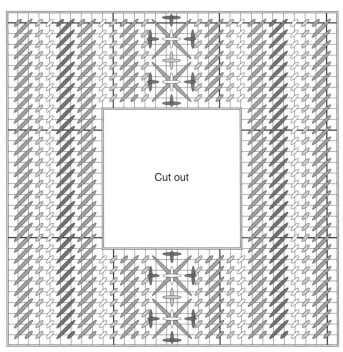

Victorian Elegance Top
31 holes x 31 holes
Cut 1

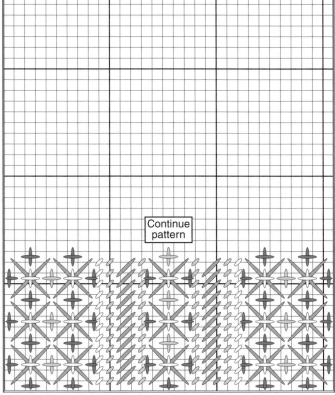

Victorian Elegance Side
31 holes x 37 holes
Cut 4

Golden Diamonds

Design by Kathy Wirth

*Combine the radiant sparkle of precious jewels with the freshest hint
of tiny flowers for a truly exquisite tissue topper!*

Skill Level: Intermediate

Size: Fits boutique-style tissue box

Materials

- 1½ sheets stiff 7-count plastic canvas
- Coats & Clark Red Heart Classic worsted weight yarn Art. E267 as listed in color key
- ⅛-inch-wide Plastic Canvas 7 Metallic Needlepoint Yarn from Rainbow Gallery yarn as listed in color key
- #16 tapestry needle
- #22 tapestry needle

Project Notes

Use #16 tapestry when stitching with yarn. Use #22 tapestry needle when working with metallic needlepoint yarn.

When working with metallic needlepoint yarn, keep yarn flat and untwisted.

Instructions

1. Cut and stitch plastic canvas according to graphs (this page and page 62).

2. Using off-white throughout, Overcast inside edges of top. Whipstitch sides A to sides B, then Whipstitch sides to top, making sure to match sides to edges on top as indicated. Overcast bottom edges. ❖

Graphs continued on page 62

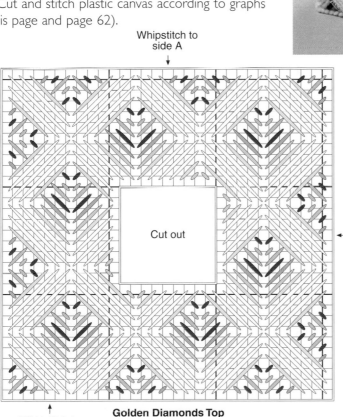

Whipstitch to side A

Whipstitch to side B

Whipstitch to side B

Cut out

Whipstitch to side A

Golden Diamonds Top
31 holes x 31 holes
Cut 1

COLOR KEY	
Worsted Weight Yarn	**Yards**
☐ Off-white #3	33
▨ Light plum #531	10
■ Dark plum #533	13
▨ Light lavender #579	5
▨ Mist green #681	10
⅛-Inch Metallic Needlepoint Yarn	
☐ Gold #PC1	20
Color numbers given are for Coats & Clark Red Heart Classic worsted weight yarn Art. E267 and Rainbow Gallery Plastic Canvas 7 Metallic Needlepoint Yarn.	

Diagonal Weave

Design by Angie Arickx

Subtle splendor abounds in this elegant tissue topper! With a unique woven design and decorative jewel-like borders, this quiet showpiece coordinates perfectly with your living room decor!

Skill Level: Intermediate

Size: Fits regular-size tissue box

Materials

- 1½ sheets 7-count plastic canvas
- Coats & Clark Red Heart Classic worsted weight yarn Art. E267 as listed in color key
- #16 tapestry needle

Instructions

1. Cut plastic canvas according to graphs (pages 55 and 56).

2. Stitch pieces following graphs, working uncoded areas with sea coral Continental Stitches.

3. Using sea coral throughout, Overcast inside edges of top and bottom edges of sides and ends. Whipstitch sides to ends, then Whipstitch sides and ends to top. ❖

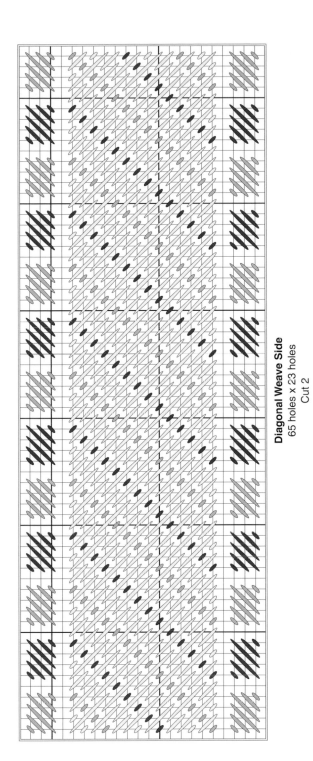

Diagonal Weave Side
65 holes x 23 holes
Cut 2

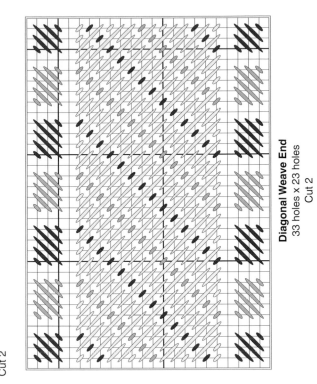

Diagonal Weave End
33 holes x 23 holes
Cut 2

COLOR KEY

Worsted Weight Yarn	Yards
☐ Sea coral #246	35
▨ Medium coral #252	11
■ Country red #914	11

Uncoded areas are sea coral
#246 Continental Stitches
Color numbers given are for Coats & Clark Red
Heart Classic worsted weight yarn Art. E267.

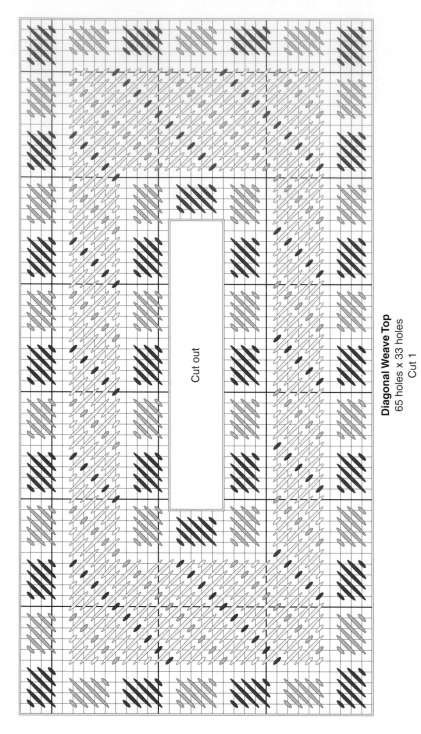

Diagonal Weave Top
65 holes x 33 holes
Cut 1

Cut out

COLOR KEY	
Worsted Weight Yarn	**Yards**
☐ Sea coral #246	35
▨ Medium coral #252	11
■ Country red #914	11
Uncoded areas are sea coral #246 Continental Stitches	

Color numbers given are for Coats & Clark Red Heart Classic worsted weight yarn Art. E267.

Art Deco

Design by Kathy Wirth

*Stately columns of black-and-white stitching surround a unique screened interior,
giving this topper a majestic touch perfect for the most elegant living room!*

Skill Level: Intermediate

Size: Fits boutique-style tissue box

Materials

- 1½ sheets stiff 7-count plastic canvas
- #3 pearl cotton as listed in color key
- ⅛-inch-wide Plastic Canvas 7 Metallic Needlepoint Yarn from Rainbow Gallery yarn as listed in color key
- #16 tapestry needle
- #20 tapestry needle
- 2 (9¼-inch x 12-inch) sheets ArtEmboss metal medium-weight aluminum from Amaco
- Wireform aluminum contour metal mesh from Amaco
- Metal-edged ruler
- Hot-glue gun

Project Notes

Use #16 tapestry when stitching with pearl cotton. Use #20 tapestry needle when working with metallic needlepoint yarn.

To cut each skein of pearl cotton into approximately 1-yard lengths, remove wrappers and untwist skein. Cut through loop that ties threads together; cut off knot. Cut through entire skein at same point.

Instructions

1. Cut plastic canvas according to graphs (page 59).

2. Using Slanted Gobelin Stitch, Cross Stitch and variation of Herringbone Stitch (above), stitch pieces with 2 strands pearl cotton (one black and one white), keeping strands flat and untwisted and keeping black strand always above white strand.

3. Overcast inside edges on top and sides with black metallic needlepoint yarn, keeping yarn flat and untwisted.

4. Using black and white pearl cotton combination, Whipstitch sides together along three of the four corners, leaving the last corner unstitched at this time; Overcast bottom edges.

5. Cut four 5 inch wide x 5¾ inch high pieces of aluminum metal and four 4½-inch-wide x 5¼-inch-high pieces of metal mesh. Center one mesh piece

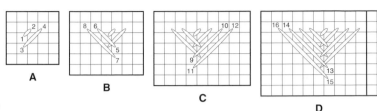

Herringbone Stitch Variation
Work each Herringbone Stitch column from
top to bottom. Start with two uppermost stitches
on right side (graph A), then work two stitches on
the left side (graph B). Work next two on right side (C),
then two on left side (D), etc., alternating down the column.

over one metal piece. Fold excess metal over ruler edge all around. Burnish metal down over mesh, covering raw edges. Repeat with remaining metal and mesh.

Continued on page 59

Southwest Quilt Block

Design by Ruby Thacker

Tried-and-true folk colors and a traditional quilt-block design lend warm country style to this mosaic topper!

following graph; turn graph 180 degrees and stitch top half.

3. Stitch half of top following graph, turn graph 180 degrees and stitch remaining half.

4. Using white throughout, Overcast inside edges of top. Whipstitch sides together, then Whipstitch sides to top. Overcast bottom edges. ❖

COLOR KEY	
Worsted Weight Yarn	**Yards**
☐ White	28
■ Burgundy	19
■ Teal blue	13
▨ Aqua	12
☐ Dusty rose	11

Skill Level: Intermediate

Size: Fits boutique-style tissue box

Materials
- 1¹/₂ sheets stiff 7-count plastic canvas
- Worsted weight yarn as listed in color key
- #16 tapestry needle

Instructions

1. Cut plastic canvas according to graphs (this page and page 59).

2. Stitch bottom half and center motif on each side

Southwest Quilt Block Side
31 holes x 37 holes
Cut 4
Stitch center and bottom half
Turn graph 180 degrees and stitch top half

COLOR KEY	
Worsted Weight Yarn	**Yards**
☐ White	28
■ Burgundy	19
■ Teal blue	13
▨ Aqua	12
☐ Dusty rose	11

Art Deco

Continued from page 57

Continued from page 57

6. Center one metal piece on wrong side of each side, with mesh facing down (mesh should be seen through openings on sides). Glue in place.

7. Using black and white pearl cotton combination, Whipstitch remaining corner of sides together, then Whipstitch sides to top. ❖

COLOR KEY	
#3 Pearl Cotton	**Yards**
☐ White and black combined	50 each
⅛-Inch Metallic Needlepoint Yarn	
╱ Black #PC11 Overcasting	16

Color number given is for Rainbow Gallery Plastic Canvas 7 Metallic Needlepoint Yarn.

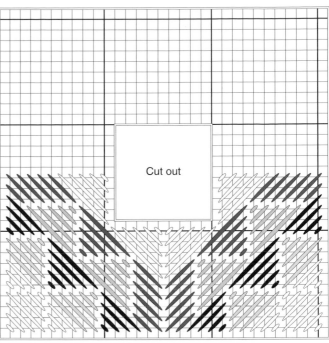

Southwest Quilt Block Top
31 holes x 31 holes
Cut 1
Stitch one half
Turn graph 180 degrees
and stitch remaining half

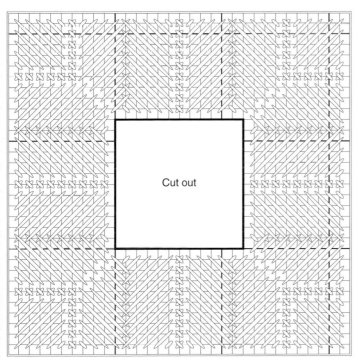

Art Deco Top
32 holes x 32 holes
Cut 1

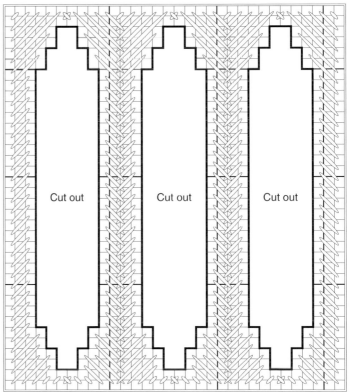

Art Deco Side
32 holes x 36 holes
Cut 4

Silver Filigree

Design by Janelle Giese

This magnificent topper glows with a sterling beauty,
making it a superb match for your living room or den!

Skill Level: Advanced

Size: Fits boutique-style tissue box

Materials

- 1½ sheets black 7-count plastic canvas
- Elmore-Pisgah Inc. Honeysuckle rayon chenille yarn as listed in color key
- Coats & Clark Red Heart Classic worsted weight yarn Art. E267 as listed in color key
- Kreinik Heavy (#32) Braid as listed in color key
- Kreinik Medium (#16) Braid as listed in color key
- #3 pearl cotton as listed in color key
- #16 tapestry needle

Project Notes

The square, triangle, heart and diamond symbols designate Continental Stitches.

When stitching with rayon chenille yarn, place 2 strands together and work with direction of nap.

Light yellow Cross Stitches are a blend of 1 strand each of Vatican gold and colonial gold medium braid.

Do not draw fibers across back of work at Whipstitch lines. This area must remain clear for assembly.

Instructions

1. Cut plastic canvas according to graphs (pages 61 and 62).

2. Leaving green highlighted Whipstitch lines on front unworked, stitch pieces following graphs, working uncoded areas on top, back and sides with slate Continental Stitches and uncoded areas on front with silver heavy braid Cross Stitches.

3. Overcast opening on top with slate. Overcast bottom edges of front, back and sides with black. On front, using Vatican gold heavy braid, Overcast cut out edges and extended edges at the top from arrow to arrow.

4. For front, use colonial gold medium braid to work Straight Stitches over completed Continental Stitches. Use a full strand black yarn to Straight Stitch center shadow at top of motif, then use Vatican gold heavy braid to work Straight Stitches over black shadow stitches.

5. Using silver heavy braid, Backstitch accents of rose, then work French Knots, wrapping each knot one time.

6. Using black pearl cotton throughout and continuing to leave green Whipstitch lines unworked until otherwise directed, work remaining embroidery on front, wrapping each silver braid French Knot, coming up and going down at same point (not graphed).

7. For sides and back, work embroidery with Vatican gold medium braid and black pearl cotton.

8. Using black yarn and Vatican gold heavy braid Whipstitch sides to front, working stitches on green Whipstitch lines as indicated. Using black, Whipstitch sides to back, then Whipstitch back and sides to top.

9. Stitch top to front along green Whipstitch lines using Continental Stitches and Cross Stitches as indicated, then work embroidery over these completed stitches. ❖

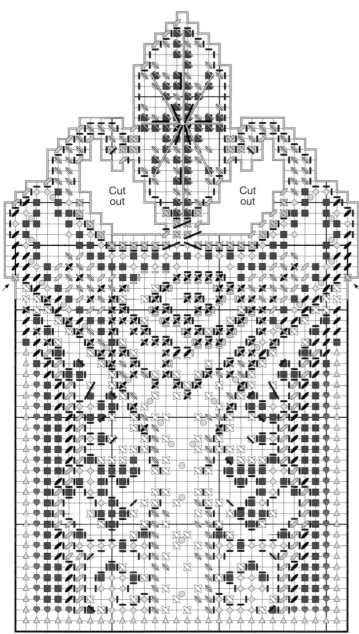

Silver Filigree Front
33 holes x 58 holes
Cut 1

COLOR KEY	
Rayon Chenille Yarn	**Yards**
■ Slate #17	110
△ Fern #20	22
♥ Moss #27	20
Uncoded areas on top, back and sides are slate #17 Continental Stitches	
Worsted Weight Yarn	
✎ Black #12	9
◇ Nickel #401	4
✎ Black #12 Straight Stitch	
Heavy (#32) Braid	
⬭ Silver #001	14
⬭ Vatican gold #102	7
Uncoded areas on front are silver #001 Cross Stitches	
⟋ Silver #001 Backstitch	
⟋ Vatican gold #102 Backstitch and Straight Stitch	
● Silver #001 French Knot	
Medium (#16) Braid	
⊠ Vatican gold #102	8
and colonial gold #104C	11
⟋ Vatican gold #102 Backstitch and Straight Stitch	
⟋ Colonial gold #104C Straight Stitch	
#3 Pearl Cotton	
⟋ Black Backstitch and Straight Stitch	15

Color numbers given are for Elmore-Pisgah Inc. rayon chenille yarn, Coats & Clark Red Heart Classic worsted weight yarn Art. E267 and Kreinik Heavy (#32) Braid and Medium (#16) Braid.

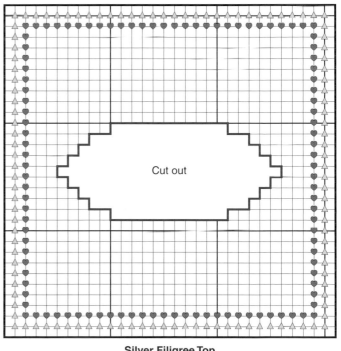

Silver Filigree Top
31 holes x 31 holes
Cut 1

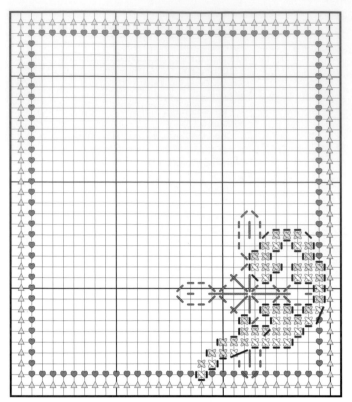

Silver Filigree Back/Side
31 holes x 36 holes
Cut 3

Golden Diamonds

Continued from page 53

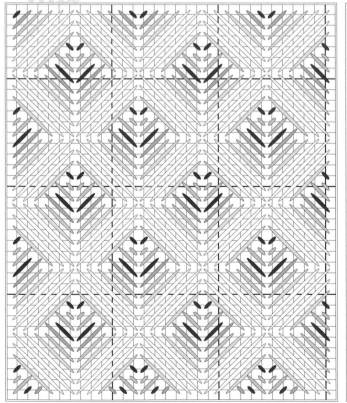

Golden Diamonds Side A
31 holes x 37 holes
Cut 2

Golden Diamond Side B
31 holes x 37 holes
Cut 2

Satin & Gold

Design by Nancy Knapp

Like a deliciously sweet dessert, this luscious confection adds taste and luxury to your decorating flair!

Skill Level: Beginner

Size: Fits boutique-style tissue box

Materials

- 1¹/₂ sheets 7-count plastic canvas
- ¹/₈-inch-wide satin ribbon as listed in color key
- DMC 6-strand metallic embroidery floss as listed in color key
- #16 tapestry needle

Project Note

Keep satin ribbon smooth and untwisted while stitching.

Instructions

1. Cut plastic canvas according to graphs.

Continued on page 65

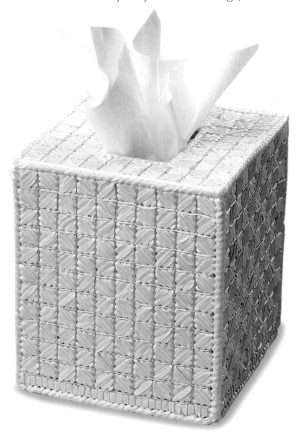

COLOR KEY	
¹/₈-Inch-Wide Satin Ribbon	**Yards**
☐ Cream	80
6-Strand Metallic Embroidery Floss	
⁄ Gold #5282 Straight Stitch	17
⁄ Gold #5282 Couching Stitch	
Color number given is for DMC 6-strand metallic embroidery floss.	

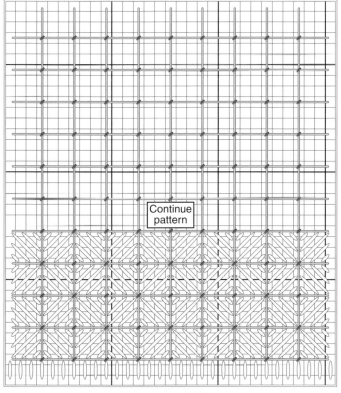

Satin & Gold Side
31 holes x 36 holes
Cut 4

Continue pattern

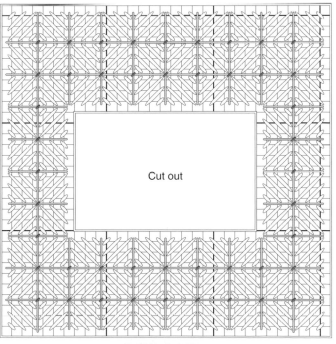

Satin & Gold Top
31 holes x 31 holes
Cut 1

Cut out

Stenciled Flowers

Design by Kathy Wirth

Full-blooming tulips and hand-painted stencils—two treasured symbols of Arts & Crafts decorating—join together for an irresistible effect in this wonderful floral topper!

Skill Level: Beginner

Size: Fits boutique-style tissue box

Materials
- 1½ sheets stiff 7-count plastic canvas
- DMC #3 pearl cotton as listed in color key
- #16 tapestry needle

Project Notes
To cut each skein of pearl cotton into approximately 1-yard lengths, remove wrappers and untwist skein. Cut through loop that ties threads together, cut off knot. Cut through entire skein at same point.

Instructions
1. Cut and stitch plastic canvas according to graphs.

2. Using 2 strands pearl cotton throughout all stitching, stitch pieces following graphs, working uncoded areas with white Continental Stitches.

3. Overcast inside edges on top with medium coral. Using white, Whipstitch sides together; then Whipstitch sides to top; Overcast bottom edges. ❖

COLOR KEY	
#3 Pearl Cotton	**Yards**
☐ White	90
■ Medium coral #350	20
▨ Coral #351	16
☐ Light coral #352	2
■ Hunter green #3346	25
▨ Medium yellow green #3347	28
☐ Light yellow green #3348	15
Uncoded areas are white	
Continental Stitches	
Color numbers given are for DMC #3 pearl cotton.	

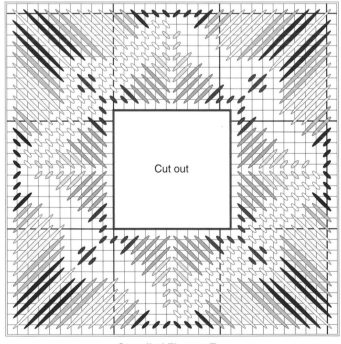

Stenciled Flowers Top
31 holes x 31 holes
Cut 1

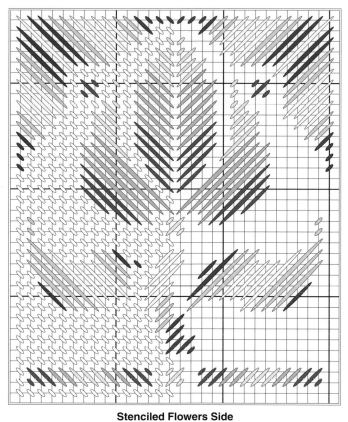

COLOR KEY

#3 Pearl Cotton	Yards
☐ White	90
■ Medium coral #350	20
▨ Coral #351	16
☐ Light coral #352	2
■ Hunter green #3346	25
▨ Medium yellow green #3347	28
☐ Light yellow green #3348	15
Uncoded areas are white	
Continental Stitches	
Color numbers given are for DMC #3 pearl cotton.	

Stenciled Flowers Side
31 holes x 37 holes
Cut 4

Satin & Gold

Continued from page 63

2. Using cream ribbon, stitch pieces following graphs.

3. Using gold metallic floss throughout, work long Straight Stitches between rows of Scotch Stitches.

Secure with Couching Stitches at corners of Scotch Stitches as indicated.

4. Using cream ribbon and a Binding Stitch throughout, Overcast inside edges of top. Whipstitch sides together, then Whipstitch sides to top. Overcast bottom edges. ❖

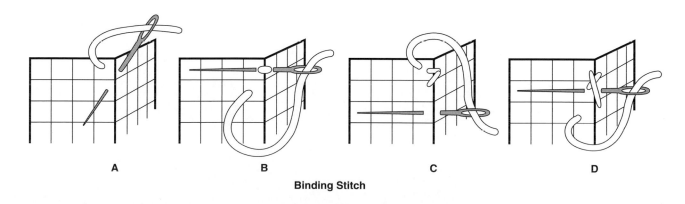

A B C D

Binding Stitch

The Dining Room

From casual summer brunches to elegant dinner parties,
it's important to arrange the dining room just right when
entertaining guests! In this chapter we offer a fabulous variety
of stylish projects guaranteed to enhance your every occasion!

Sweet Sunflower

Design by Susan Leinberger

Bold and beautiful, this bright and cheery topper creates an unmistakable atmosphere of summer fun!

Skill Level: Beginner

Size: Fits boutique-style tissue box

Materials

- 2 sheets 7-count plastic canvas
- Uniek Needloft plastic canvas yarn as listed in color key
- #16 tapestry needle
- Hot-glue gun

Instructions

1. Cut plastic canvas according to graphs (this page and page 78).

2. Stitch sides and top following graphs, working holly Straight Stitches and brown French Knots when background stitching is completed.

3. Overcast flower centers with brown, then work French Knots.

4. Stitch remaining pieces following graphs. Overcast each petal with yellow, Whipstitching edges of dart together while Overcasting. Work embroidery and Overcast stems and leaves with forest.

5. Using photo as a guide, glue eight flower petals around edges on backside of each flower center. Glue stems, leaves and flowers to sides A, allowing room for Overcasting and Whipstitching.

6. Using holly throughout, Overcast inside edges of top and bottom edges of sides. Whipstitch sides A to sides B, then Whipstitch sides to top. ❖

COLOR KEY	
Plastic Canvas Yarn	**Yards**
■ Red #01	55
■ Brown #15	20
▨ Holly #27	18
□ Yellow #57	30
⟋ Holly #27 Straight Stitch	
⟋ Forest #29 Backstitch Straight Stitch and Overcasting	3
● Brown #15 French Knot	
● Gold #17 French Knot	2
Color numbers given are for Uniek Needloft plastic canvas yarn.	

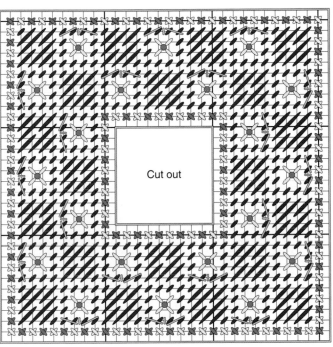

Sweet Sunflower Top
31 holes x 31 holes
Cut 1

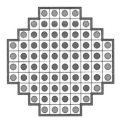

Sweet Sunflower Center
10 holes x 10 holes
Cut 2

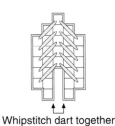

Whipstitch dart together

Sweet Sunflower Petal
5 holes x 8 holes
Cut 16

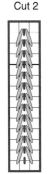

Sweet Sunflower Stem
3 holes x 14 holes
Cut 2

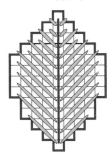

Sweet Sunflower Leaf
9 holes x 13 holes
Cut 4

Graphs continued on page 78

Patchwork Pinwheels

Design by Angie Arickx

With its interesting quilt pattern and fresh colors choices, this intriguing topper will draw plenty of second looks as it graces your table or sideboard!

Skill Level: Beginner

Size: Fits boutique-style tissue box

Materials
- 1½ sheets 7-count plastic canvas
- Uniek Needloft plastic canvas yarn as listed in color key
- #16 tapestry needle

Instructions

1. Cut and stitch plastic canvas according to graphs (this page and page 79).

2. Using moss throughout, Overcast bottom edges of sides and inside edges of top. Whipstitch sides together, then Whipstitch sides to top. ❖

COLOR KEY	
Plastic Canvas Yarn	**Yards**
☐ Moss #25	17
■ Forest #29	31
☐ Eggshell #39	23
☐ Lilac #45	4
■ Purple #46	25
Color numbers given are for Uniek Needloft plastic canvas yarn.	

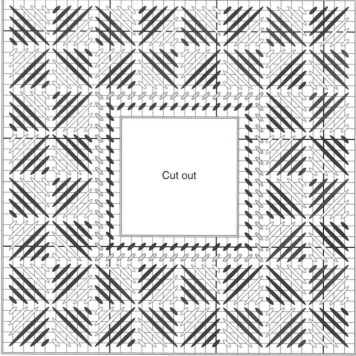

Patchwork Pinwheels Top
33 holes x 33 holes
Cut 1

Graphs continued on page 79

Elegant Fruit Basket

Design by Janelle Giese

*Let the abundant delights of nature's bounty overflow into your home
from the fruitful baskets of this graceful topper!*

Skill Level: Intermediate

Size: Fits boutique-style tissue box

Materials

- 1½ sheets black 7-count plastic canvas
- Uniek Needloft plastic canvas yarn as listed in color key
- Elmore-Pisgah Inc. Honeysuckle rayon chenille yarn as listed in color key
- Kreinik Medium (#16) Braid as listed in color key
- Kreinik ⅛-inch metallic ribbon as listed in color key
- #3 pearl cotton as listed in color key
- #16 tapestry needle

Project Notes

The square, triangle, inverted triangle, heart and diamond symbols represent Continental Stitches.

When stitching with rayon chenille yarn, place two strands together and work with direction of nap.

Keep metallic ribbon and medium braid flat and untwisted while stitching.

Instructions

1. Cut plastic canvas according to graphs (this page and page 79).

2. Stitch pieces following graphs, working metallic ribbon stitches first and working uncoded areas with hunter Continental Stitches. Overcast opening on top with black rayon chenille yarn.

3. When background stitching is completed, work mallard Backstitches along antique gold borders. Use antique gold to work Straight Stitches over stitches on basket where indicated.

4. Backstitch dent of peach with lichen. Straight Stitch apple highlight and work Pin Stitches for grape highlights with light pink.

5. Straight Stitch apple stem with cinnamon, then work black pearl cotton Straight Stitch under stem. Complete all remaining embroidery on sides with black pearl cotton.

6. Using black rayon chenille yarn, Whipstitch sides together, then Whipstitch sides to top; Overcast bottom edges. ❖

Graphs continued on page 79

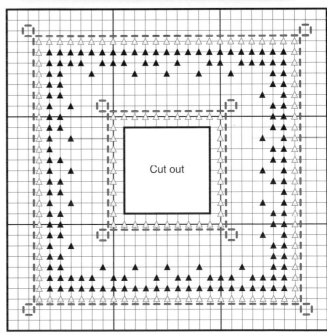

Elegant Fruit Basket Top
30 holes x 30 holes
Cut 1

Cross Stitch Fantasy

Design by Susan Leinberger

Ivory blooms float freely on the petal-toned surface of this delicately smocked topper, giving your home the freshness of eternal spring!

Skill Level: Intermediate

Size: Fits regular-size tissue box

Materials

- 2 sheets ivory 7-count plastic canvas
- Uniek Needloft solid metallic craft cord as listed in color key
- Uniek Needloft plastic canvas yarn as listed in color key
- #16 tapestry needle
- 2 (1³/₄-inch) ivory #810 ribbon petal roses from C.M. Offray & Son Inc.
- 6 (⁷/₈-inch) cream #815 ribbon asters from C.M. Offray & Son Inc.
- Hot-glue gun

Instructions

1. Cut plastic canvas according to graphs.

2. Stitch pieces following graphs, working the Trellis Cross Stitch Variation following diagram given

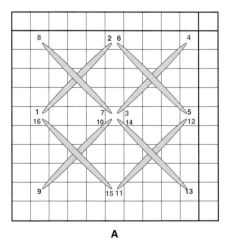

A

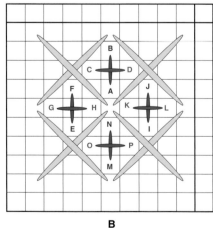

B

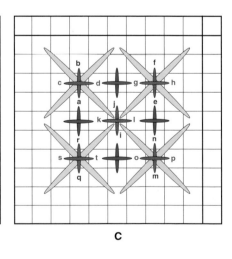

C

Trellis Cross Stitch Variation

Following graph A, work large Cross Stitches horizontally, coming up at 1, down at 2, up at 3, down at 4, etc.
Following graph B, work forest Upright Cross Stitches next, coming up at A, down at B, up at C, down at D, etc.
Following graph C, work purple Upright Cross Stitches last, coming up at a, down at b, up at c, down at d, etc.

and filling in at top, bottom and sides of this pattern stitch as indicated.

3. Using eggshell throughout, Overcast inside edges of top and bottom edges of sides and ends. Whipstitch sides to ends, then Whipstitch sides and ends to top.

4. Using photo as a guide, glue ribbon flowers to top. ❖

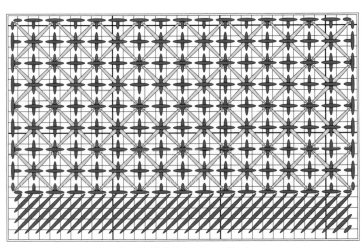

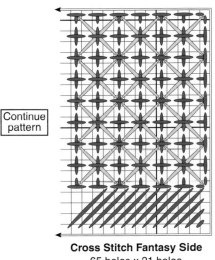

Continue pattern

Cross Stitch Fantasy Side
65 holes x 21 holes
Cut 2

Cross Stitch Fantasy End
33 holes x 21 holes
Cut 2

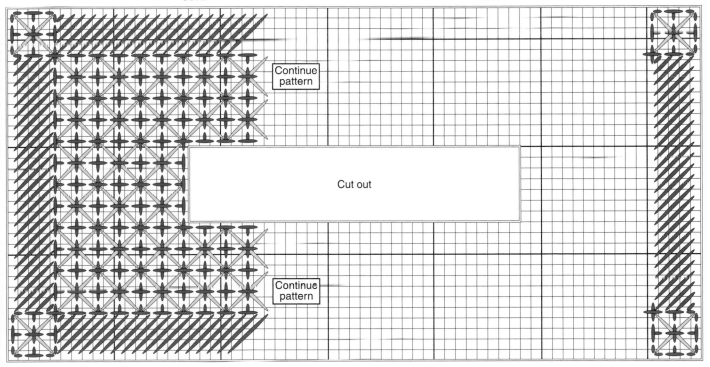

Continue pattern

Cut out

Continue pattern

Cross Stitch Fantasy Top
65 holes x 33 holes
Cut 1

Study in Blue

Design by Ruby Thacker

You'll love the way these shades of blue crisscross each other in an intricate pattern that will complement your finest china!

Skill Level: Intermediate

Size: Fits boutique-style tissue box

Materials
- 1½ sheets 7-count plastic canvas
- Coats & Clark Red Heart Super Saver worsted weight yarn Art. E300 as listed in color key
- #16 tapestry needle

Instructions

1. Cut plastic canvas according to graphs (this page and page 80).

2. Stitch pieces following graphs, working the Trellis Cross Stitch Variation following diagram given (page 70), working light blue Cross Stitches first, skipper blue Upright Stitches next and soft navy Upright Cross Stitches last.

3. Using skipper blue throughout, Overcast inside edges of top and bottom edges of sides and ends. Whipstitch sides together, then Whipstitch sides to top. ❖

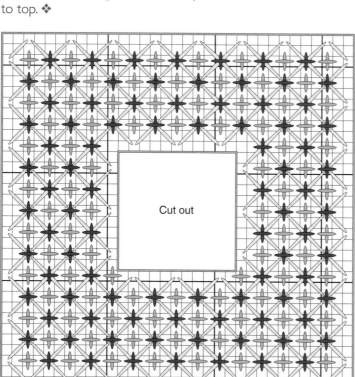

Study in Blue Top
33 holes x 33 holes
Cut 1

COLOR KEY	
Worsted Weight Yarn	**Yards**
☐ Light blue #381	28
▨ Skipper blue #384	27
■ Soft navy #387	20
Color numbers given are for Coats & Clark Red Heart Super Saver worsted weight yarn Art. E300.	

Graphs continued on page 80

Elegant Plaid

Design by Maryanne Moreck

With its jaunty tassels and modern color scheme, this choice topper says "tartan" with a twist!

Skill Level: Beginner

Size: Fits boutique-style tissue box

Materials

- 1½ sheets 7-count plastic canvas
- Coats & Clark Red Heart Classic worsted weight yarn Art. E267 as listed in color key
- ⅛-inch-wide Plastic Canvas 7 Metallic Needlepoint Yarn by Rainbow Gallery as listed in color key
- #16 tapestry needle
- 20 (½-inch) white pearl buttons with shanks
- Hand-sewing needle
- White sewing thread
- 2½-inch square heavy cardboard

Instructions

1. Cut plastic canvas according to graphs (this page and page 80).

2. Stitch pieces following graphs, working uncoded areas with white Continental Stitches.

3. Using hand-sewing needle and white sewing thread,

attach five buttons to bottom border of each side where indicated.

4. Using silver worsted weight yarn throughout, Overcast inside edges of top and bottom edges of sides. Whipstitch sides together, then Whipstitch sides to top.

5. Wrap silver worsted weight yarn around cardboard 15 times. For hanger, slip a 10-inch length of silver under wraps at top, tying off securely. Cut through loops at bottom.

6. Wrap a 10-inch length silver metallic needlepoint yarn around tassel approximately ⅝ inch from top

Continued on page 80

COLOR KEY

Worsted Weight Yarn	Yards
☐ Silver #412	41
Uncoded areas are white	
#1 Continental Stitches	18
⅛-Inch Metallic Needlepoint Yarn	
☐ Silver #PC2	8
● Attach button	

Color numbers given are for Coats & Clark Red Heart Classic worsted weight yarn Art. E267 and Rainbow Gallery Plastic Canvas 7 Metallic Needlepoint Yarn.

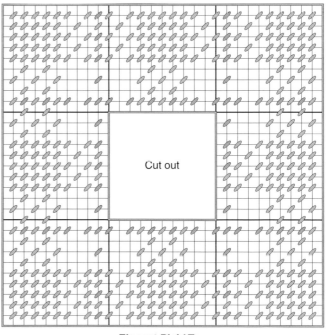

Elegant Plaid Top
30 holes x 30 holes
Cut 1

English Cottage

Design by Angie Arickx

The friendly down-home charm of this pastel-painted cottage will put all your guests in the mood for a good old-fashioned country meal!

Skill Level: Intermediate

Size: Fits boutique-style tissue box

Materials

- 2 sheets 7-count plastic canvas
- Uniek Needloft plastic canvas yarn as listed in color key
- #16 tapestry needle
- Hot-glue gun

Cutting & Stitching

1. Cut plastic canvas according to graphs (pages 75, 76 and 77). Cut two 2-hole x 7-hole pieces for small shutters and 12 (2-hole x 12-hole) pieces for large shutters.

2. Continental Stitch and Overcast shutters with camel. Following graphs throughout all stitching, stitch and Overcast window boxes and front steps. Stitch all remaining pieces, leaving blue Whipstitch lines on cottage back unworked.

3. When background stitching is completed, work mermaid Straight Stitches for flower stems. Work yellow French Knots for flowers and gray French Knot for door knob, wrapping needle one time.

4. Using beige, Overcast top and bottom edges of cottage front and sides; Overcast top edge of back and bottom edges of back from each bottom corner to blue dot.

5. Using sail blue, Overcast bottom edges of roof and vertical edges of chimney openings; Overcast bottom edges of eaves from arrow to arrow.

6. Using lavender, Overcast top edges of chimney, inside edges of fence, top edges of fence from dot to dot, and all bottom edges of fence except extreme bottom edges of posts.

Assembly

1. Using lavender through step 2, Whipstitch chimney pieces together along side edges. Whipstitch back edge of fence bottom to cottage back between blue dots.

2. Whipstitch fence sides to cottage back along blue Whipstitch lines, then Whipstitch fence sides to fence

front. Whipstitch bottom of fence posts to fence bottom, Overcasting remaining edges of bottom while Whipstitching.

3. Using beige, Whipstitch cottage front and back to sides.

4. Using sail blue, Whipstitch top edges of roof pieces together, then Whipstitch bottom edges of two chimney sides to horizontal edges of chimney opening. **Note:** *The last two bottom edges of chimney sides will remain unstitched.* Whipstitch eaves to roof sides.

5. Using photo as a guide through step 6, glue small shutters and one window box to sides and bottom of small window on front. Glue large shutters and remaining window boxes to sides and bottom of all large windows.

6. Center and glue front steps under door on cottage front, making sure bottom edges are even. Glue roof to top of cottage. ❖

COLOR KEY

Plastic Canvas Yarn	Yards
▨ Lavender #05	25
☐ Sail blue #35	40
▨ Gray #38	2
☐ Beige #40	65
▨ Camel #43	9
■ Dark royal #48	4
▨ Mermaid #54	4
✎ Mermaid #54 Straight Stitch	
● Gray #38 French Knot	
○ Yellow #57 French Knot	2

Color numbers given are for Uniek Needloft plastic canvas yarn.

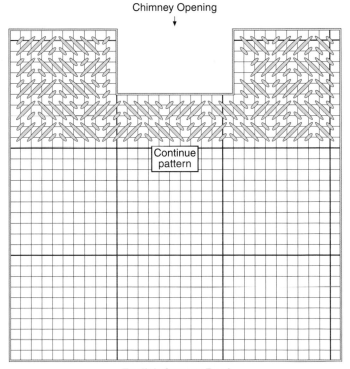

Chimney Opening

Continue pattern

English Cottage Roof
31 holes x 31 holes
Cut 2

English Cottage Front Steps
13 holes x 7 holes
Cut 1

English Cottage Window Box
7 holes x 3 holes
Cut 7

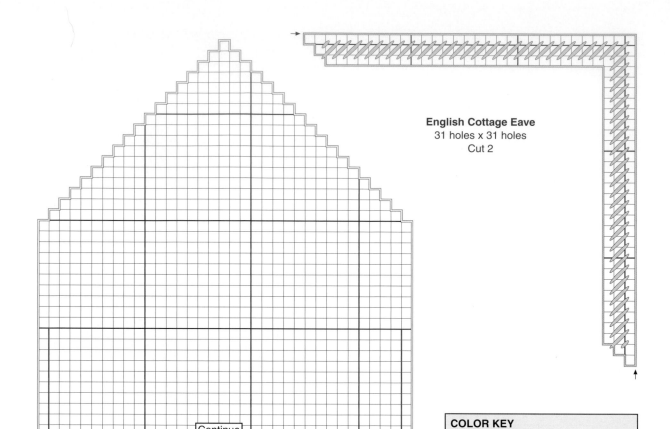

English Cottage Eave
31 holes x 31 holes
Cut 2

English Cottage Back
35 holes x 47 holes
Cut 1

Continue pattern

COLOR KEY	
Plastic Canvas Yarn	**Yards**
☐ Lavender #05	25
☐ Sail blue #35	40
☐ Gray #38	2
☐ Beige #40	65
☐ Camel #43	9
☐ Dark royal #48	4
☐ Mermaid #54	4
╱ Mermaid #54 Straight Stitch	
● Gray #38 French Knot	
○ Yellow #57 French Knot	2
Color numbers given are for Uniek Needloft plastic canvas yarn.	

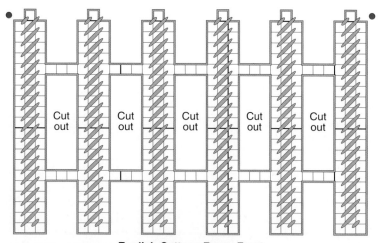

Cut out Cut out Cut out Cut out Cut out

English Cottage Fence Front
33 holes x 21 holes
Cut 1

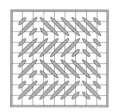

English Cottage Chimney
9 holes x 9 holes
Cut 4

Back Edge

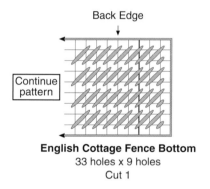

Continue
pattern

English Cottage Fence Bottom
33 holes x 9 holes
Cut 1

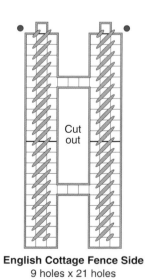

Cut
out

English Cottage Fence Side
9 holes x 21 holes
Cut 2

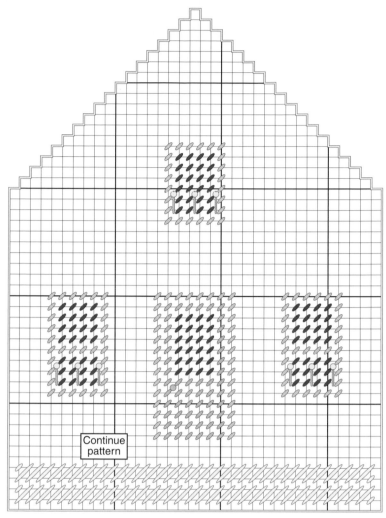

Continue
pattern

English Cottage Front
35 holes x 47 holes
Cut 1

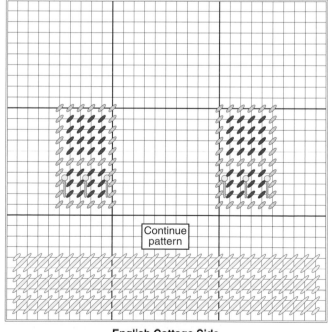

Continue
pattern

English Cottage Side
30 holes x 30 holes
Cut 2

Sweet Sunflower

Continued from page 67

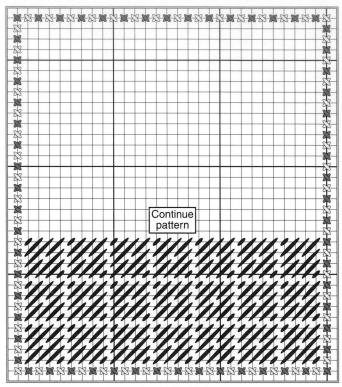

COLOR KEY	
Plastic Canvas Yarn	**Yards**
■ Red #01	55
■ Brown #15	20
☐ Holly #27	18
☐ Yellow #57	30
⁄ Holly #27 Straight Stitch	
⁄ Forest #29 Backstitch	
Straight Stitch and Overcasting	3
● Brown #15 French Knot	
● Gold #17 French Knot	2
Color numbers given are for Uniek Needloft plastic canvas yarn.	

Sweet Sunflower Side A
31 holes x 35 holes
Cut 2

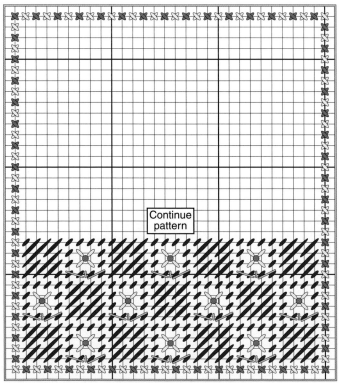

Sweet Sunflower Side B
31 holes x 35 holes
Cut 2

Patchwork Pinwheels

Continued from page 68

Continued from page 68

COLOR KEY	
Plastic Canvas Yarn	**Yards**
☐ Moss #25	17
■ Forest #29	31
☐ Eggshell #39	23
☐ Lilac #45	4
■ Purple #46	25
Color numbers given are for Uniek Needloft plastic canvas yarn.	

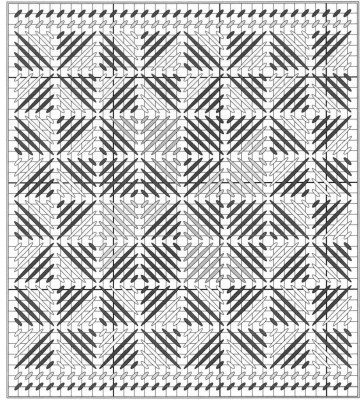

Patchwork Pinwheels Side
33 holes x 37 holes
Cut 4

Elegant Fruit Basket

Continued from page 69

Continued from page 69

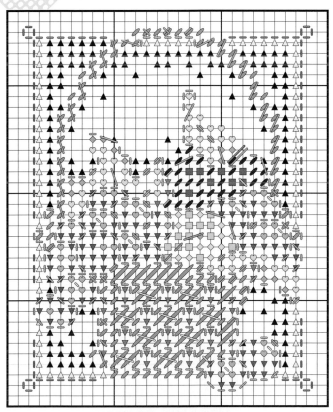

Elegant Fruit Basket Side
30 holes x 37 holes
Cut 4

COLOR KEY	
Plastic Canvas Yarn	**Yards**
⬗ Maple #13	11
▼ Cinnamon #14	4
⬗ Cinnamon #14 Straight Stitch	
Rayon Chenille Yarn	
◇ Light pink #6	5
☐ Pumpkin #8	3
♡ Fern #20	9
■ Red #22	3
⬗ Ruby #23	5
◆ Lichen #26	6
▲ Black #30	42
♥ Dark plum #46	10
▼ Blackberry #49	16
Uncoded areas are hunter #19 Continental Stitches	73
⬗ Light pink #6 Straight Stitch and Pin Stitch	
⬗ Lichen #26 Backstitch	
⅛-Inch Metallic Ribbon	
△ Antique gold #205C	11
⬗ Antique gold #205C Straight Stitch	
Medium (#16) Braid	
⬗ Mallard #850 Backstitch	9
#3 Pearl Cotton	
⬗ Black Backstitch and Straight Stitch	22
Color numbers given are for Uniek Needloft plastic canvas yarn, Elmore Pisgah Inc. rayon chenille yarn and Kreinik ⅛-inch Ribbon and Medium (#16) Braid.	

Study In Blue
Continued from page 72

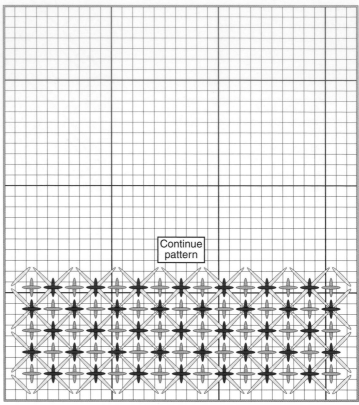

COLOR KEY
Worsted Weight Yarn	Yards
☐ Light blue #381	28
☒ Skipper blue #384	27
■ Soft navy #387	20

Color numbers given are for Coats & Clark Red Heart Super Saver worsted weight yarn Art. E300.

Continue pattern

Study in Blue Side
33 holes x 37 holes
Cut 4

Elegant Plaid
Continued from page 73

fold and tie off securely; trim ends. Trim tassel ends so they are even. Repeat three more times.

7. Thread one tassel hanger through each top corner, allowing tassel to hang about ³/8-inch from corner; secure hanger under yarn on wrong side. ❖

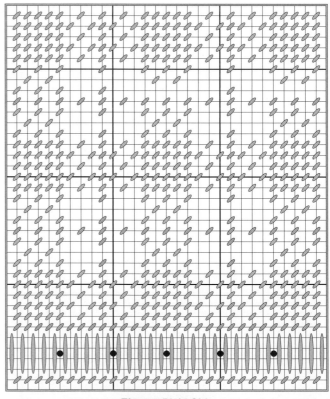

COLOR KEY
Worsted Weight Yarn	Yards
☐ Silver #412	41
Uncoded areas are white #1 Continental Stitches	18
✎x-Inch Metallic Needlepoint Yarn	
☐ Silver #PC2	8
● Attach button	

Color numbers given are for Coats & Clark Red Heart Classic worsted weight yarn Art. E267 and Rainbow Gallery Plastic Canvas 7 Metallic Needlepoint Yarn.

Elegant Plaid Side
30 holes x 36 holes
Cut 4

The Bathroom

From the master bath to the guest bath, this is one room that demands an extra-fresh, extra-cheerful decorating scheme! In this chapter you'll find a delightful variety of breezy, beautiful projects to brighten up any bathroom in your home!

Stylized Flowers

Design by Kathy Wirth

This multicultural piece combines the bright pastels of western skies with the sculptured beauty of traditional Eastern art for a truly diplomatic accent!

Skill Level: Beginner

Size: 10¼ inches W × 5⅝ inches H × 6¼ inches D (fits boutique-style tissue box and one roll bathroom tissue)

Materials

- 2½ sheets stiff 7-count plastic canvas
- Coats & Clark Red Heart Classic worsted weight yarn Art. E267 as listed in color key
- Coats & Clark Red Heart Super Saver worsted weight yarn Art. E301 as listed in color key
- Coats & Clark Anchor #3 pearl cotton as listed in color key
- #16 tapestry needle
- ½ sheet white self-adhesive Presto felt from Kunin Felt
- Hot-glue gun

Project Note

For clarification, the top is used on the facial tissue side of the topper. The lid and base are used on the bathroom tissue side of the topper.

Instructions

1. Cut plastic canvas according to graphs (this page and pages 83 and 84). Cut one 38-hole-wide × 37-hole-high piece for divider. Divider and base will remain unstitched.

2. Cut white felt slightly smaller all around than lid. Set aside.

3. Stitch ends, working one as graphed and one replacing mist green Continental Stitches with blue jewel Continental Stitches.

4. Stitch corners, top, lid and sides, working two corners

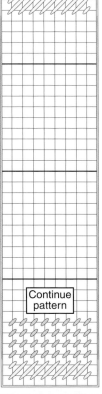

Stylized Flowers Corner
9 holes x 37 holes
Cut 4
Stitch 2 as graphed
Stitch 2 replacing mist green
with blue jewel

as graphed and two replacing mist green with blue jewel.

5. When background stitching is completed, work dark avocado Backstitches on sides and ends.

6. Overcast inside edges of top with white. Using maize, Whipstitch from dot to dot around left side of lid, leaving right side unworked at this time.

Assembly

1. Using adjacent colors throughout, Whipstitch blue corners to right sides of ends and green corners to left sides.

2. Using maize through step 4, Whipstitch unstitched base to bottom left side of assembled topper, leaving right edge of base unworked at this time.

3. Whipstitch top to top right side of assembled topper, leaving left edge of top unworked at this time.

4. Overcast remaining top and bottom

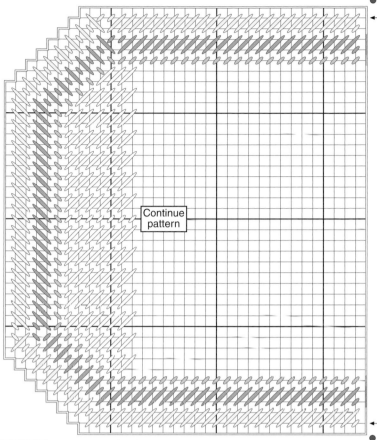

Continue pattern

Stylized Flowers Lid & Base
34 holes x 40 holes
Cut 2
Stitch 1 as graphed for lid
Do not stitch base

edges of topper. Whipstitch one 38-hole edge of divider to base between arrows.

5. Place top edge of divider between arrows on left side of top, then using adjacent colors, Whipstitch divider, top and lid together through all three thicknesses.

6. Adhere felt to wrong side of lid. ❖

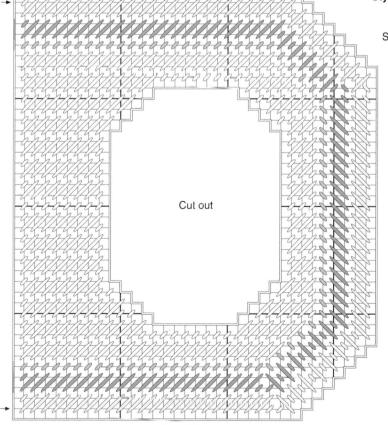

Cut out

Stylized Flowers Top
34 holes x 40 holes
Cut 1

COLOR KEY	
Worsted Weight Yarn	**Yards**
☐ White #1	32
▨ Sea coral #246	14
☐ Maize #261	26
■ Artichoke #391	8
▨ Light lavender #579	15
▨ Mist green #681	30
▨ Blue jewel #818	30
#3 Pearl Cotton	
╱ Dark avocado #269 Backstitch	4
Color numbers given are for Coats & Clark Red Heart Classic worsted weight yarn Art. E207 and Super Saver worsted weight yarn Art. E301, and Anchor #3 pearl cotton.	

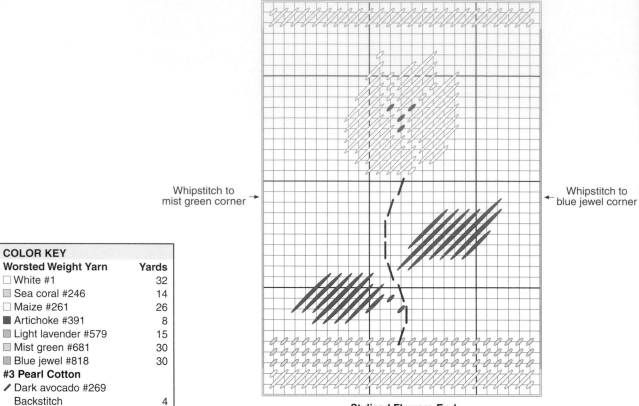

Whipstitch to
mist green corner →

← Whipstitch to
blue jewel corner

COLOR KEY

Worsted Weight Yarn	Yards
☐ White #1	32
☐ Sea coral #246	14
☐ Maize #261	26
■ Artichoke #391	8
☐ Light lavender #579	15
☐ Mist green #681	30
☐ Blue jewel #818	30

#3 Pearl Cotton

╱ Dark avocado #269	
Backstitch	4

Color numbers given are for Coats &
Clark Red Heart Classic worsted weight
yarn Art. E267 and Super Saver worsted
weight yarn Art. E301, and Anchor #3
pearl cotton.

Stylized Flowers End
26 holes x 37 holes
Cut 2
Stitch 1 as graphed
Stitch 1 replacing mist green Continental Stitches
with blue jewel Continental Stitches

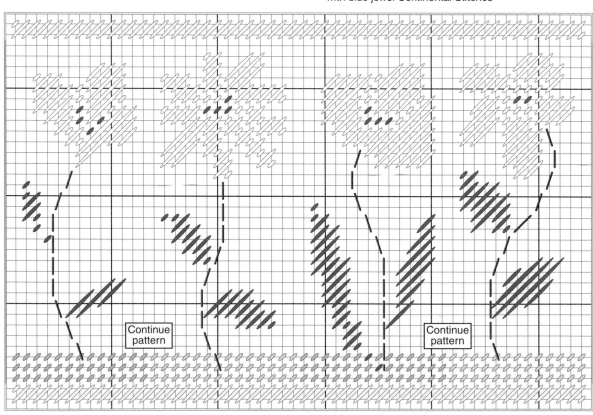

Continue
pattern

Continue
pattern

Stylized Flowers Side
55 holes x 37 holes
Cut 2

Sea Horse Duo

Designs by Ruby Thacker

*Stately sea horses swim around the sides of this
shell-adorned nautical set!*

Skill Level: Intermediate

Size

Bathroom Tissue Topper: 5³/₄ inches H x 4⁷/₈ inches in diameter

Facial Tissue Topper: Fits boutique-style tissue box

Materials

- 2¹/₂ sheets 7-count plastic canvas
- 6-inch plastic canvas radial circle
- Coats & Clark Red Heart Classic worsted weight yarn Art. E267 as listed in color key
- Uniek Needloft solid metallic craft cord as listed in color key
- DMC 6-strand metallic embroidery floss as listed in color key
- #16 tapestry needle

Bathroom Tissue Cover

1. Cut sides from plastic canvas according to graphs; cut one plastic canvas radial circle for top, cutting away gray area (pages 86, 87 and 88).

2. Using light sage, stitch top as graphed. Overlap four holes on ends of sides forming one 102-hole circle. Stitch with yarn as graphed, working uncoded areas with light sage Continental Stitches.

3. Remove string from center of solid gold cord, then stitch shells, working the three center stitches last.

4. Using 2 strands gold metallic embroidery floss, work Backstitches to outline sea horses.

5. Using light sage, Whipstitch side to top; Overcast bottom edge.

Facial Tissue Topper

1. Cut plastic canvas according to graphs (pages 86 and 87).

2. Stitch pieces following graphs, working uncoded areas with light sage Continental Stitches.

3. Remove string from center of solid gold cord, then stitch shells, working the three center stitches last.

4. Using 2 strands gold metallic embroidery floss, work Backstitches around sea horses.

5. Using light sage, Overcast inside edges of top and bottom edges of sides. Whipstitch sides together, then Whipstitch sides to top. ❖

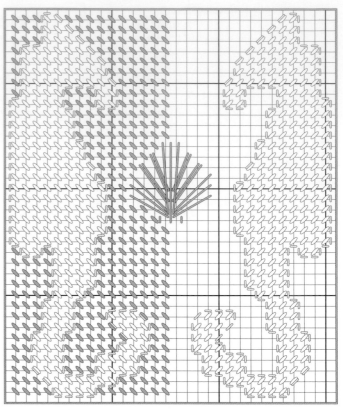

Sea Horse Duo Facial Tissue Topper Side
31 holes x 37 holes
Cut 4

COLOR KEY	
Worsted Weight Yarn	**Yards**
☐ White #1	48
▨ Light sage #631	92
Uncoded areas are light sage #631 Continental Stitches	
Solid Metallic Craft Cord	
⁄ Solid gold #55020 Straight Stitch	7
6-Strand Metallic Embroidery Floss	
⁄ Gold #5282 Backstitch	9
Color numbers given are for Coats & Clark Red Heart Classic worsted weight yarn Art. E267, Uniek Needloft solid metallic craft cord and DMC 6-strand metallic embroidery floss.	

Overlap   Overlap

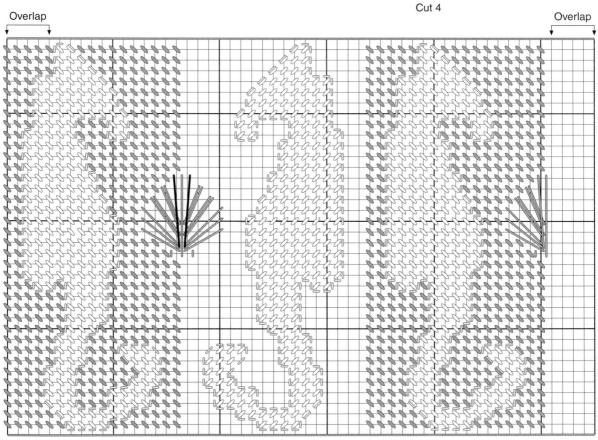

Sea Horse Duo Bathroom Tissue Topper Side A
55 holes x 37 holes
Cut 1

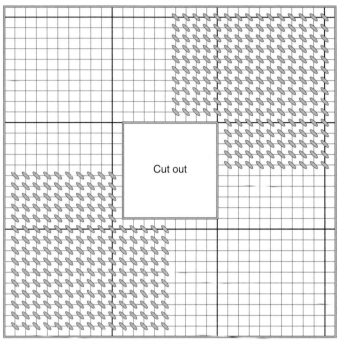

Sea Horse Duo Facial Tissue Topper Top
31 holes x 31 holes
Cut 1

Overlap   Overlap

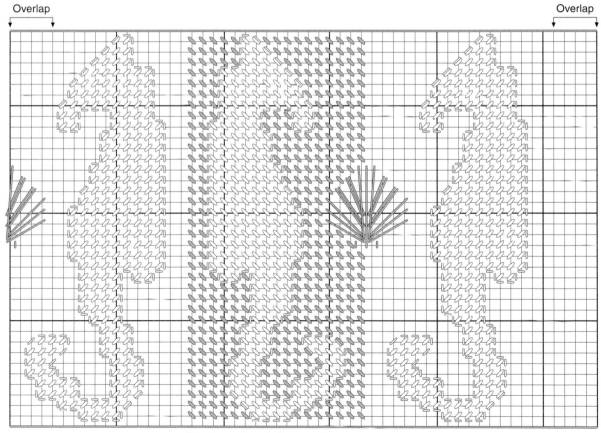

Sea Horse Duo Bathroom Tissue Topper Side B
55 holes x 37 holes
Cut 1

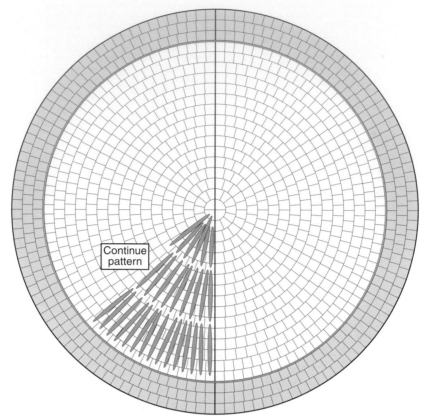

Sea Horse Duo Bathroom Tissue Topper Top
Cut 1 from radial circle,
cutting away gray area

COLOR KEY	
Worsted Weight Yarn	**Yards**
□ White #1	48
▨ Light sage #631	92
Uncoded areas are light sage #631 Continental Stitches	
Solid Metallic Craft Cord	
✎ Solid gold #55020 Straight Stitch	7
6-Strand Metallic Embroidery Floss	
✎ Gold #5282 Backstitch	9
Color numbers given are for Coats & Clark Red Heart Classic worsted weight yarn Art. E267, Uniek Needloft solid metallic craft cord and DMC 6-strand metallic embroidery floss.	

Daisies on Blue

Design by Kathy Wirth

You'll love the way this cheerful project combines classic blue-and-white coloration with flower-power retro patterning!

Skill Level: Beginner

Size: Fits regular-size tissue box

Materials

- 2 sheets stiff 7-count plastic canvas
- Coats & Clark Red Heart Classic worsted weight yarn Art. E267 as listed in color key
- #16 tapestry needle
- 10 (9mm) round sapphire #X661-020 cabochons from The Beadery
- Jewel glue

Instructions

1. Cut plastic canvas according to graphs (pages 90 and 91).

2. Stitch pieces following graphs, working uncoded areas on white background with true blue Continental Stitches. Uncoded areas with pink background will remain unstitched.

3. When background stitching is completed, work Lazy Daisy Stitches with white.

4. Overcast inside edges on top with white. Following graphs, Whipstitch sides to ends, then Whipstitch sides and ends to top. Overcast bottom edges with white.

5. Glue one cabochon to center of each daisy where indicated on graphs. ❖

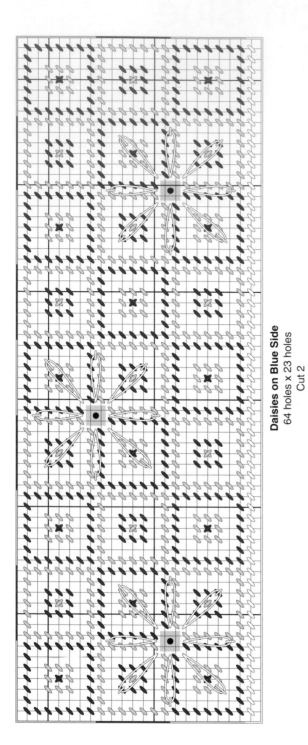

Daisies on Blue Side
64 holes x 23 holes
Cut 2

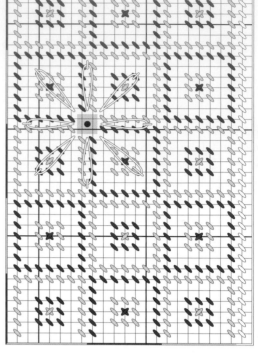

Daisies on Blue End
34 holes x 23 holes
Cut 2

COLOR KEY	
Worsted Weight Yarn	**Yards**
☐ White #1	16
☐ Blue jewel #818	36
■ Soft navy #853	26
Uncoded areas on white background are true blue #822 Continental Stitches	33
⌀ White #1 Lazy Daisy Stitch	
● Attach cabochon	
Color numbers given are for Coats & Clark Red Heart Classic worsted weight yarn Art. E267.	

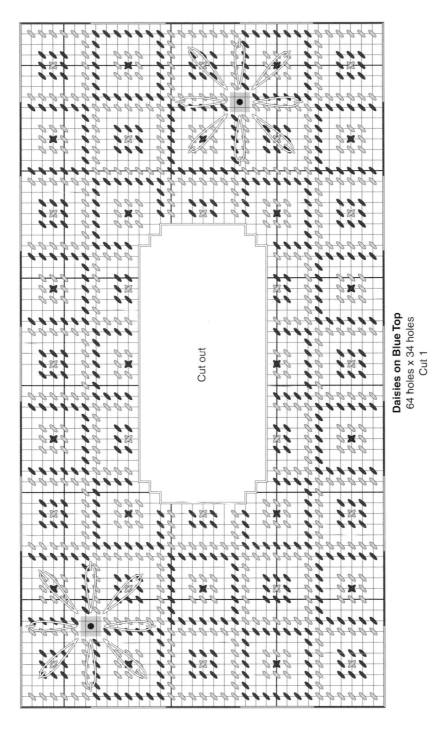

Daisies on Blue Top
64 holes x 34 holes
Cut 1

Cut out

COLOR KEY	
Worsted Weight Yarn	**Yards**
☐ White #1	16
☐ Blue jewel #818	36
■ Soft navy #853	26
Uncoded areas on white background are true blue #822 Continental Stitches	33
◌ White #1 Lazy Daisy Stitch	
● Attach cabochon	

Color numbers given are for Coats & Clark Red Heart
Classic worsted weight yarn Art. E267.

Egret Bay

Design by Janelle Giese

*Handsome and elegant, this stately egret pauses at the water's edge
to lend graceful calm to your bathroom decor!*

Project Note

The square, triangle, inverted triangle, heart and diamond shapes on egret motif graph are Continental Stitches.

Instructions

1. Cut topper pieces from black 7-count plastic canvas; cut egret motif from clear 10-count plastic canvas according to graphs (pages 93 and 94).

2. Continental Stitch egret motif following graph, working uncoded areas with dark blue green Continental Stitches; work very light drab brown Cross Stitch for eye. Overcast motif with Vatican gold.

3. When background stitching is completed, Straight Stitch outer feather lines with very light gray green. Work black #3 and #8 pearl cotton embroidery as indicated.

4. Following Fig. 1 and using black #8 pearl cotton, work pupil of eye on very light drab brown Cross Stitch.

5. Stitch top, front, back and sides of topper, working uncoded areas on front and top with black yarn Continental Stitches. Work corner motifs on top and Wheat Stitch Variation on all topper pieces following diagrams given (page 94).

6. Using black #5 pearl cotton, center and attach egret motif to front by Backstitching around edges as indicated.

Skill Level: Advanced

Size: Fits boutique-style tissue box

Materials

- 1¹/₂ sheets black 7-count plastic canvas
- ¹/₂ sheet clear 10-count plastic canvas
- Coats & Clark Red Heart Classic worsted weight yarn Art. E267 as listed in color key
- Kreinik Medium (#16) Braid as listed in color key
- DMC #3 pearl cotton as listed in color key
- DMC #5 pearl cotton as listed in color key
- DMC #8 pearl cotton as listed in color key
- #16 tapestry needle

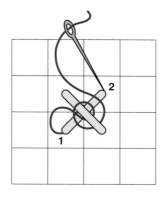

Fig. 1
Bring #8 pearl cotton up at lower left corner
of Cross Stitch (1). Wrap around top stitch,
pulling snugly; draw back down at upper
right corner of Cross Stitch (2).

7. Using black yarn throughout, Overcast inside edges of top and bottom edges of front, back and sides. Whipstitch front and back to sides, then Whipstitch front, back and sides to top. ❖

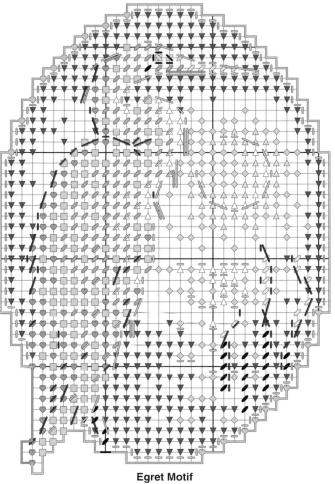

Egret Motif
31 holes x 44 holes
Cut 1 from clear 10-count

COLOR KEY	
Worsted Weight Yarn	**Yards**
⬮ Black #12	40
⬮ Seafoam #684	19
⬮ Windsor blue #808	34
⬮ Country blue #882	3
Uncoded areas on top and front are black #12 Continental Stitches	
Medium (#16) Braid	
♥ Vatican gold #102	40
⬮ Vatican gold #102 Backstitch and Straight Stitch	
#3 Pearl Cotton	
⬮ Black #310	4
◆ Medium blue green #503	2
⬮ Very light drab brown #613	1
△ Off white #746	1
▼ Very dark gray green #924	5
♥ Medium gray green #926	2
◻ Light gray green #927	2
⬮ Very light gray green #928	2
△ Light Nile green #955	1
Uncoded areas on egret motif are dark blue green #501 Continental Stitches	3
⟋ Black #310 Backstitch	
⬮ Very light gray green #928 Straight Stitch	
#5 Pearl Cotton	
⬮ Black #310 Backstitch	2
#8 Pearl Cotton	
⟋ Black #310 Backstitch and Straight Stitch	2
Color numbers given are for Coats & Clark Red Heart Classic worsted weight yarn Art. E267, Kreinik Medium (#16) Braid and DMC #3, #5 and #8 pearl cotton.	

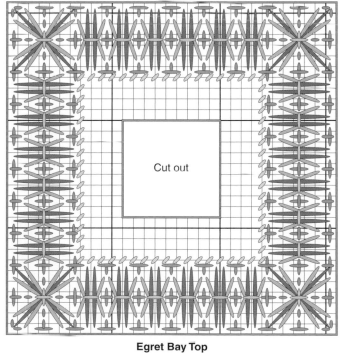

Egret Bay Top
31 holes x 31 holes
Cut 1 from black 7-count

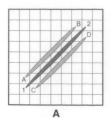 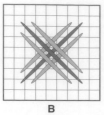 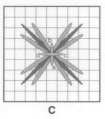

A	B	C

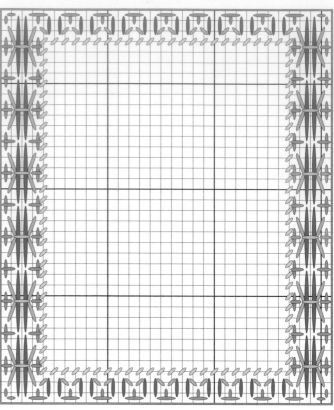

Egret Bay Corner Motif

Work three diagonal stitches with Windsor blue and seafoam as in graph A. Next work three diagonal stitches going in opposite direction, always working stitches so top diagonal stitches point toward center of piece. Following graph C, work Vatican gold stitches, coming up at a, down at b, etc.

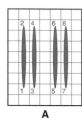 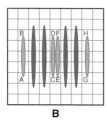 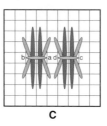

A	B	C

Wheat Stitch Variation

Following graph A, work stitches with Windsor blue, coming up at 1, down at 2, up at 3, down at 4, etc. Work seafoam stitches in graph B next, coming up at A, down at B, etc. Following graph C, work Vatican goldstitches last, coming up at a, down at b, etc.

Egret Bay Front
31 holes x 37 holes
Cut 1 from black 7-count

COLOR KEY	
Worsted Weight Yarn	**Yards**
Black #12	40
Seafoam #684	19
Windsor blue #808	34
Country blue #882	3
Uncoded areas on top and front are black #12 Continental Stitches	
Medium (#16) Braid	
Vatican gold #102	40
Vatican gold #102 Backstitch and Straight Stitch	
#3 Pearl Cotton	
Black #310	4
Medium blue green #503	2
Very light drab brown #613	1
Off white #746	1
Very dark gray green #924	5
Medium gray green #926	2
Light gray green #927	2
Very light gray green #928	2
Light Nile green #955	1
Uncoded areas on egret motif are dark blue green #501 Continental Stitches	3
Black #310 Backstitch	
Very light gray green #928 Straight Stitch	
#5 Pearl Cotton	
Black #310 Backstitch	2
#8 Pearl Cotton	
Black #310 Backstitch and Straight Stitch	2

Color numbers given are for Coats & Clark Red Heart Classic worsted weight yarn Art. E267, Kreinik Medium (#16) Braid and DMC #3, #5 and #8 pearl cotton.

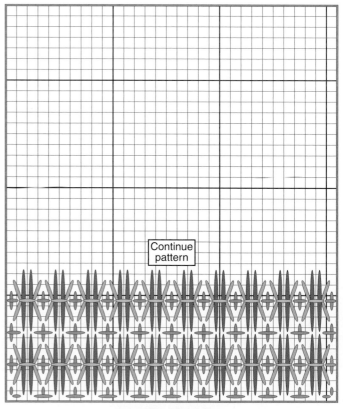

Continue pattern

Egret Bay Side & Back
31 holes x 37 holes
Cut 3 from black 7-count

Squares in Squares

Design by Kathy Wirth

*Bold and breathtaking, this striking topper will set a vibrant tone
for a distinctly different decorating style!*

Skill Level: Beginner

Size: Fits boutique-style tissue box

Materials

- 1½ sheets stiff 7-count plastic canvas
- Coats & Clark Red Heart Classic worsted weight yarn Art. E267 as listed in color key
- Coats & Clark Red Heart Super Saver worsted weight yarn Art. E300 as listed in color key
- #16 tapestry needle

Instructions

1. Cut and stitch plastic canvas according to graphs (this page and page 101).

2. Overcast inside edges of top and bottom edges of sides with black.

3. Using adjacent colors, Whipstitch sides together, then Whipstitch sides to top. ❖

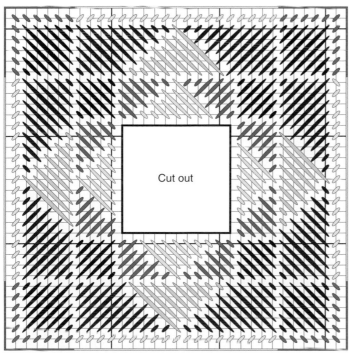

Squares in Squares Top
32 holes x 32 holes
Cut 1

COLOR KEY	
Worsted Weight Yarn	**Yards**
▢ Sea coral #246	13
■ Black #312	27
▢ Pale green #363	20
▨ Teal #388	16
■ Country red #914	20
Color numbers given are for Coats & Clark Red Heart Classic worsted weight yarn Art. E267 and Super Saver worsted weight yarn Art. E300.	

Graphs continued on page 101

Sea Treasures

Design by Janelle Giese

You'll be dreaming of warm sandy beaches and cool coral reefs
when you decorate with this breezy nautical accent!

Skill Level: Advanced

Size: Fits boutique-style tissue box

Materials

- 2 sheets almond 7-count plastic canvas
- 1½ sheets clear stiff 7-count plastic canvas
- Worsted weight yarn as listed in color key
- Kreinik Medium (#16) Braid as listed in color key
- 2 yards copper #021C Kreinik Cord
- DMC #5 pearl cotton as listed in color key
- #16 tapestry needle
- 30 Mill Hill Products medium nutmeg #82053 glass bugle beads from Gay Bowles Sales Inc.
- 6 (4mm) crystal rhinestones

- ⅞-inch brass-plated cup hook
- Sawtooth hanger
- Beading needle
- Carpet thread
- Thick white glue

Project Note

For back and each side, place one clear stiff piece behind one almond piece, then stitch as one.

Cutting & Stitching

1. Cut one front, one back, two sides, one lid top, four shells and two rim ends from almond plastic canvas; cut one back and two sides from clear stiff plastic canvas according to graphs (pages 97, 98, 99 and 100).

2. Cut one 28-hole x 5-hole piece from almond plastic canvas for lid rim front. Cut one 30-hole x 30-hole piece each from almond and clear stiff plastic canvas for base. Base, lid rim front and lid rim ends will remain unstitched.

3. Leaving green highlighted Whipstitch lines unworked, stitch top, working uncoded areas with off-white Continental Stitches. Overcast edges with light tan, leaving back edge between blue dots unworked.

4. For each shell, place two pieces together and stitch as one. Overcast edges with light terra-cotta.

5. Stitch back as graphed, leaving red and blue highlighted Whipstitch lines and area between them unworked. Using light tan, Overcast both top and bottom edges from arrow to arrow.

6. Stitch shell motifs on sides with off-white as graphed, reversing pieces for one side before stitching and leaving red highlighted Whipstitch line and blue shaded areas unworked at this time. Work light tan stitches over off-white stitches. Overcast top edges with light tan.

7. Leaving orange highlighted Whipstitch lines

unworked, stitch front piece following graph, working uncoded areas with off-white Continental Stitches and working yarn Straight Stitches on shell as part of background stitching. Work light terra-cotta stitches at bottom of shell motif first, then work light tan stitches over terra-cotta stitches.

8. When background stitching is completed, use 1 ply light sage yarn to embroider leaves at top. Using beading needle and copper cord, attach bugle beads where indicated, stitching through beads two times.

9. Work curry braid Backstitches and Straight Stitches, then work all pearl cotton embroidery. Overcast top edge with tan and extended edges with light sage and medium sage.

Assembly

1. Using light tan, Whipstitch front edges of sides to front, working medium sage Continental Stitches at orange Whipstitch lines.

2. Placing clear base piece on top of almond base piece, Whipstitch base pieces to bottom edge of front with light tan.

3. Attach base to sides at red line by working

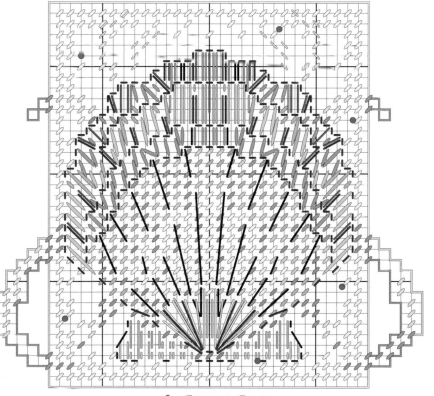

Sea Treasures Front
40 holes x 36 holes
Cut 1 from almond

COLOR KEY	
Worsted Weight Yarn	**Yards**
☐ Off-white	55
☐ Light tan	37
▨ Light terra-cotta	5
■ Medium terra-cotta	3
▨ Pale rose	3
☐ Light sage	3
■ Medium sage	2
■ Light rose	2
▨ Medium rose	1
■ Medium tan	1
☐ Light gold	1
Uncoded areas on front and top are off-white Continental Stitches	
⁄ Light tan Straight Stitch	
⁄ Light terra-cotta Straight Stitch	
⁄ Medium terra-cotta Straight Stitch	
⁄ Pale rose Straight Stitch	
⁄ Light sage (1-ply) Backstitch and Straight Stitch	
⁄ Light rose Straight Stitch	
Medium (#16) Braid	
⁄ Curry #2122 Backstitch and Straight Stitch	4
#5 Pearl Cotton	
⁄ Dark beige brown #839 Straight Stitch	2
⁄ Attach bugle bead	
● Attach rhinestone	
○ Attach cup hook	
Color numbers given are for Kreinik Medium (#16) Braid and DMC #5 pearl cotton.	

off-white stitches for shells in blue highlighted areas first; complete shell motifs with light tan.

4. Using light tan throughout, Whipstitch base to back at red line; Whipstitch sides to back along unworked side edges. Overcast bottom edges of sides.

5. Using off-white, Whipstitch side edges of lid rim front to lid rim ends where indicated. Using off-white and light tan, Continental Stitch top edge of assembled lid rim to lid top at green highlighted lines.

6. Using light tan, Whipstitch back edge of lid top between blue dots to blue line on back.

7. Using carpet thread, sew sawtooth hanger to center back of assembled topper near top edge.

8. Using photo as a guide, center and glue one shell to back above topper and one to lower bottom of back below topper. Where indicated on shell graph, screw cup hook into bottom shell, going through back.

9. Glue rhinestones to front where indicated on graph. ❖

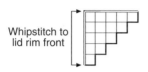

Sea Treasures Lid Rim End
5 holes x 5 holes
Cut 2 from almond
Do not stitch

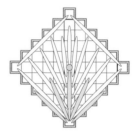

Sea Treasures Shell
11 holes x 11 holes
Cut 4 from almond

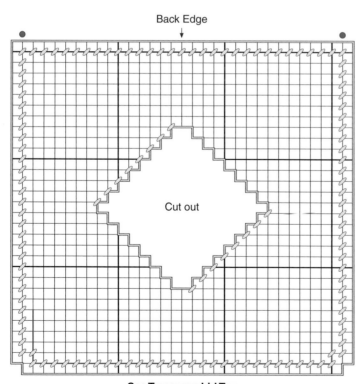

Back Edge

Cut out

Sea Treasures Lid Top
32 holes x 31 holes
Cut 1 from almond

COLOR KEY	
Worsted Weight Yarn	**Yards**
☐ Off-white	55
☐ Light tan	37
☐ Light terra-cotta	5
■ Medium terra-cotta	3
☐ Pale rose	3
☐ Light sage	3
■ Medium sage	2
■ Light rose	2
☐ Medium rose	1
■ Medium tan	1
☐ Light gold	1
Uncoded areas on front and top are off-white Continental Stitches	
╱ Light tan Straight Stitch	
╱ Light terra-cotta Straight Stitch	
╱ Medium terra-cotta Straight Stitch	
╱ Pale rose Straight Stitch	
╱ Light sage (1-ply) Backstitch and Straight Stitch	
╱ Light rose Straight Stitch	
Medium (#16) Braid	
╱ Curry #2122 Backstitch and Straight Stitch	4
#5 Pearl Cotton	
╱ Dark beige brown #839 Straight Stitch	2
╱ Attach bugle bead	
● Attach rhinestone	
○ Attach cup hook	
Color numbers given are for Kreinik Medium (#16) Braid and DMC #5 pearl cotton.	

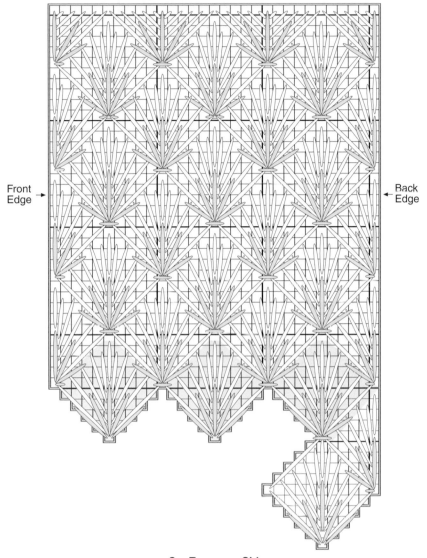

Front
Edge →

← Back
Edge

Sea Treasures Side
31 holes x 51 holes
Cut 2 each from almond and clear stiff
Reverse 1 each of almond
and clear stiff before stitching

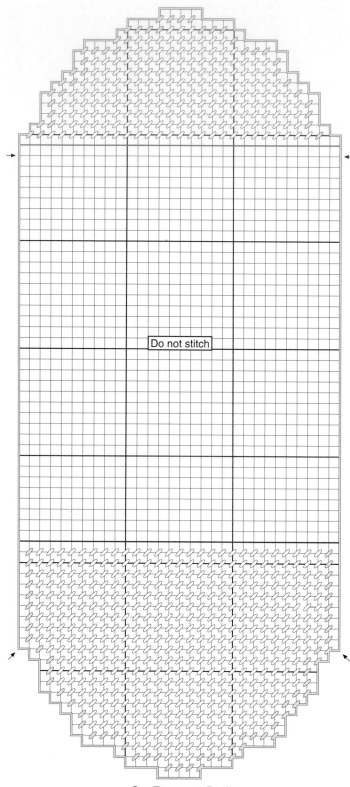

Sea Treasures Back
30 holes x 72 holes
Cut 1 each from almond and clear stiff

Do not stitch

Squares in Squares Side
32 holes x 37 holes
Cut 4

COLOR KEY	
Worsted Weight Yarn	**Yards**
☐ Sea coral #246	13
■ Black #312	27
☐ Pale green #363	20
■ Teal #388	16
■ Country red #914	20
Color numbers given are for Coats & Clark Red Heart Classic worsted weight yarn Art. E267 and Super Saver worsted weight yarn Art. E300.	

The Master Bedroom

Whether it's the grandest room in your home, or your coziest personal retreat, the assortment of projects in this chapter will help you decorate the master bedroom with just the right balance of elegance and style!

Cosmetics Caddy

Design by Susan Leinberger

Perky and practical, this charming floral topper is designed for classy convenience!

Skill Level: Intermediate

Size: $5^3/_4$-inches W × $5^7/_8$-inches H × $8^3/_4$ inches D (fits boutique-style tissue box)

Materials

- 3 sheets clear 7-count plastic canvas
- $^1/_2$ sheet almond 7-count plastic canvas
- 4-inch Uniek QuickShape plastic canvas radial circle
- Uniek Needloft plastic canvas yarn as listed in color key
- #16 tapestry needle

Instructions

1. Cut plastic canvas radial circle in half along center line for pocket base; cut one pocket front liner from almond plastic canvas; cut all remaining pieces from clear plastic canvas according to graphs (this page and pages 104 and 122).

2. Cut one 28-hole × 12-hole piece for organizer base. Both base pieces and pocket front liner will remain unstitched.

3. Stitch remaining pieces following graphs, working uncoded areas on topper front and back and on caddy and organizer fronts with watermelon Continental Stitches. Blue highlighted Whipstitch lines will remain unstitched at this time.

4. When background stitching is completed, work burgundy Backstitches and yellow French Knots.

5. Overcast inside edges of top with burgundy.

COLOR KEY	
Plastic Canvas Yarn	**Yards**
■ Burgundy #03	20
□ Pink #07	3
▨ Sandstone #16	25
□ Moss #25	6
■ Holly #27	6
□ Flesh tone #56	65
▨ Yellow #57	3
Uncoded areas are watermelon #55 Continental Stitches	10
✒ Burgundy #03 Backstitch	
⊙ Yellow #57 French Knot	
Color numbers given are for Uniek Needloft plastic canvas yarn.	

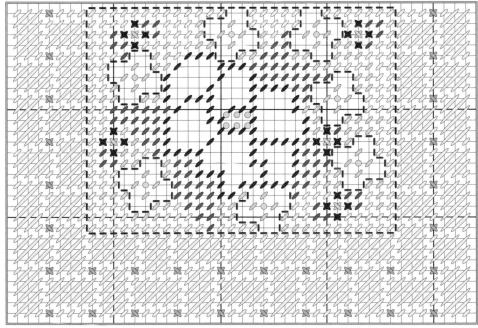

Cosmetics Caddy Pocket Front
44 holes x 30 holes
Cut 1 from clear
Stitch as graphed
Cut 1 from almond for lining
Do not stitch

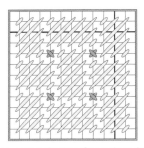

Cosmetics Caddy Organizer Side
12 holes x 12 holes
Cut 2 from clear

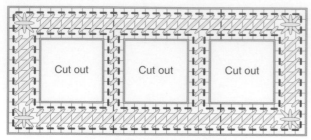

Cosmetics Caddy Organizer Top
28 holes x 12 holes
Cut 1 from clear

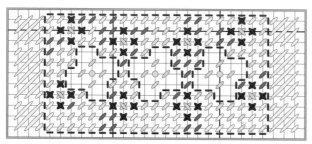

Cosmetics Caddy Organizer Front
28 holes x 12 holes
Cut 1 from clear

Using sandstone through step 8, Overcast inside edges of organizer top and bottom edges of caddy front and back.

6. Place almond pocket front liner behind stitched pocket front, then Whipstitch top edges together. Whipstitch pocket sides to side A where indicated with blue lines, working through all three thicknesses. Whipstitch pocket base to bottom edges of side A and pocket front.

Graphs and text continued on page 122

COLOR KEY	
Plastic Canvas Yarn	**Yards**
■ Burgundy #03	20
□ Pink #07	3
▨ Sandstone #16	25
▨ Moss #25	6
■ Holly #27	6
□ Flesh tone #56	65
□ Yellow #57	3
Uncoded areas are watermelon #55 Continental Stitches	10
╱ Burgundy #03 Backstitch	
○ Yellow #57 French Knot	
Color numbers given are for Uniek Needloft plastic canvas yarn.	

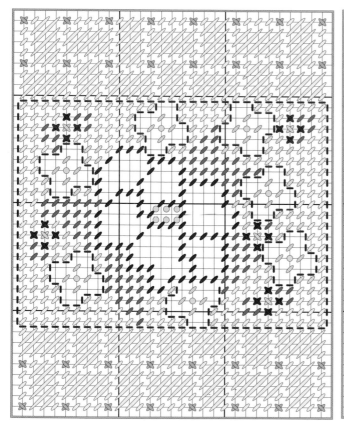

Cosmetics Caddy Front & Back
30 holes x 38 holes
Cut 2 from clear

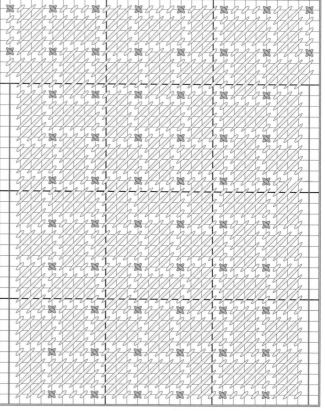

Cosmetics Caddy Side A
30 holes x 38 holes
Cut 1 from clear

White Roses on Amethyst

Design by Angie Arickx

Add a delicate feminine touch to your nightstand or dresser with this light-as-air floral accent!

Skill Level: Beginner

Size: Fits boutique-style tissue box

Materials

- 1½ sheets 7-count plastic canvas
- Uniek Needloft plastic canvas yarn as listed in color key
- #16 tapestry needle

Instructions

1. Cut plastic canvas according to graphs (this page and page 121).

2. Stitch pieces following graphs, working uncoded areas with purple Continental Stitches.

3. Using purple throughout, Overcast inside edges of top and bottom edges of sides. Whipstitch sides together; then Whipstitch sides to top. ❖

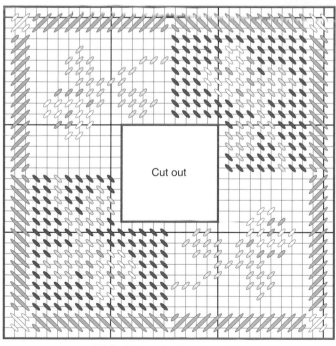

White Roses on Amethyst Top
31 holes x 31 holes
Cut 1

COLOR KEY	
Plastic Canvas Yarn	**Yards**
☐ Silver #37	10
☐ Gray #38	5
☐ White #41	12
☐ Lilac #45	21
■ Purple #46	52
Uncoded areas are purple #46 Continental Stitches	
Color numbers given are for Uniek Needloft plastic canvas yarn.	

Graphs continued on page 121

Leafy Glade

Design by Terry Ricioli

You can almost hear the rustling of these softly falling leaves
as they nestle together in their bamboo frames!

Skill Level: Beginner

Size: Fits boutique-style tissue box

Materials

- 1¹/₂ sheets 7-count plastic canvas
- Uniek Needloft plastic canvas yarn as listed in color key
- #16 tapestry needle

Instructions

1. Cut plastic canvas according to graphs.

2. Stitch pieces following graphs, working uncoded areas with eggshell Continental Stitches.

3. Using camel throughout, Overcast inside edges of top. Whipstitch sides together, turning two sides 180 degrees and placing them on opposite sides before Whipstitching. Whipstitch sides to top. Overcast bottom edges. ❖

COLOR KEY	
Plastic Canvas Yarn	**Yards**
☐ Fern #23	16
■ Christmas green #28	20
☐ Camel #43	15
Uncoded areas are eggshell	
#39 Continental Stitches	50
Color numbers given are for Uniek Needloft plastic canvas yarn.	

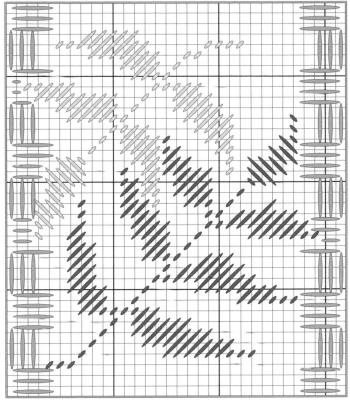

Leafy Glade Side
32 holes x 37 holes
Cut 4

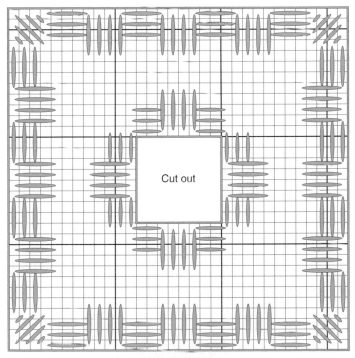

Cut out

Leafy Glade Top
32 holes x 32 holes
Cut 1

Stack-n-Stitch Jewel Tone

Design by Kathy Wirth

With its stunning shaped pieces and distinctly dynamic flavor, this is one home accent that is sure to stand out with style!

Skill Level: *Advanced*

Size: Fits boutique-style tissue box

Materials

- 6 sheets white 7-count plastic canvas
- 1/16-inch-wide Plastic Canvas 10 Metallic Needlepoint Yarn by Rainbow Gallery as listed in color key
- DMC #3 pearl cotton as listed in color key
- #16 tapestry needle
- #18 tapestry needle
- 20 (10mm) square dark fuchsia #X640-085 acrylic faceted stones from The Beadery
- 24-gauge gold craft wire #2490-212 from The Beadery
- 12 inches 3/16-inch dowel
- Wire cutters
- Small pliers
- Nylon strapping tape
- Jewel glue

Project Notes

Use #16 tapestry needle with pearl cotton and #18 tapestry needle with metallic needlepoint yarn.

To cut pearl cotton skeins into 15 lengths approximately 1 yard each in length, remove wrappers, open skein to form loop, cut through thread that holds strands together, then cut through all strands at same point, cutting off knot.

Keep gold metallic needlepoint yarn flat and smooth while stitching.

When adding layers, always make sure canvas holes are properly aligned. Small pieces of nylon strapping tape may be used to anchor first few thread tails on back. Do not stitch through tape.

Sides

1. Following cutting diagram for side squares (page 109), cut 16 (16-hole × 16-hole) pieces for layer 1. Cut 32 each of the following: layer 2, 14 holes × 14 holes; layer 3, 12 holes × 12 holes; layer 4, 10 holes × 10 holes; layer 5, 8 holes × 8 holes; layer 6, 6 holes × 6 holes; layer 7, 4 holes × 4 holes.

2. Following stitch diagrams (page 110) for the 16 side squares (eight each of stacked squares A and B), center two layer 2 squares on one layer 1 square and work one gold stitch through all three layers on one side only.

3. Center two layer 3 squares on top of layer 2 squares and work one gold stitch on same side, working through all five layers.

4. Continue in this manner, centering next smallest pair of squares on top of the stack and

working gold stitches through all layers. After centering layer 6 squares on stack (no gold stitches on this layer), immediately center layer 7 squares on top and work last gold stitch on that side.

5. When layers 1 through 7 are stacked, work remaining gold stitches and pearl cotton stitches through all layers.

6. Cut 24 (15-inch) lengths from wire. Wrap each length around dowel. Push wraps close together, forming springlike coil; remove dowel.

7. Position all squares with outside colors matching (see photo). With four squares making up each side, connect squares following step 8 until all four sides are joined together.

8. Holding two squares with wrong sides together and aligning edges, twist coil wire through outer row of holes, making sure no holes are missed. Straighten excess wire at each corner. Trim wire ends to about 1 inch; bend to wrong side. Anchor wire ends with nylon strapping tape.

Top

1. Following cutting diagram for top corner squares (page 110), cut four (16-hole x 16-hole) pieces for layer 1. Cut eight each of the following: layer 2, 14 holes x 14 holes; layer 3, 12 holes x 12 holes; layer 4, 10 holes x 10 holes; layer 5, 8 holes x 8 holes; layer 6, 6 holes x 6 holes; layer 7, 4 holes x 4 holes.

2. Following stitch diagrams (page 110) for each of the four corners (two each of stacked squares A and B), stack two layer 2 squares on one layer 1 square and work one small gold stitch on one side.

3. Continue stacking and stitching, following instructions in steps 3 through 5 for sides.

4. Cut four 10-inch lengths from wire. Wrap each length around dowel following instructions in step 6 for sides.

5. Following steps 7 and 8 for sides, join corners along 8-hole edges.

Final Assembly

1. Cut eight 15-inch lengths and four 30-inch lengths from wire. Wrap each length around dowel following instructions in step 6 for sides.

2. Following steps 7 and 8 for sides, attach top to sides using 15-inch lengths wire. Add wire to bottom edges of sides using 30-inch lengths.

3. Glue one acrylic faceted stone to top of each stack. ❖

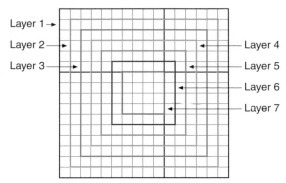

**Stack-n-Stitch Jewel Tone
Side Squares Cutting Diagram**

Layer 1 (black lines)
16 holes x 16 holes
Cut 16

Layer 2 (pink lines)
14 holes x 14 holes
Cut 32

Layer 3 (blue lines)
12 holes x 12 holes
Cut 32

Layer 4 (orange lines)
10 holes x 10 holes
Cut 32

Layer 5 (green lines)
8 holes x 8 holes
Cut 32

Layer 6 (red lines)
6 holes x 6 holes
Cut 32

Layer 7 (purple lines)
4 holes x 4 holes
Cut 32

COLOR KEY	
$^1/_{16}$-Inch Metallic Needlepoint Yarn	**Yards**
☐ Gold #PM51	30
#3 Pearl Cotton	
✏ Ultra dark pistachio green	
#890 Straight Stitch	35
✏ Very dark mauve	
#3685 Straight Stitch	35
Color numbers given are for Rainbow Gallery Plastic Canvas 10 Metallic Needlepoint Yarn and DMC #3 pearl cotton.	

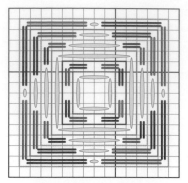

**Stack-n-Stitch Jewel Tone
Side Square A Stitch Diagram**
Stitch 8

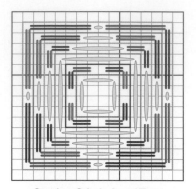

**Stack-n-Stitch Jewel Tone
Side Square B Stitch Diagram**
Stitch 8

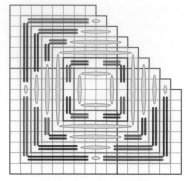

**Stack-n-Stitch Jewel Tone
Top Corner Square A Stitch Diagram**
Stitch 2

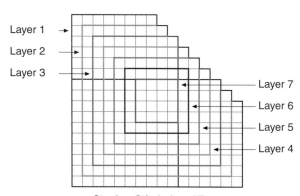

**Stack-n-Stitch Jewel Tone
Top Corner Squares Cutting Diagram**

Layer 1 (black lines)
16 holes x 16 holes
Cut 4

Layer 2 (pink lines)
14 holes x 14 holes
Cut 8, cutting out along
7-hole black diagonal edge

Layer 3 (blue lines)
12 holes x 12 holes
Cut 8, cutting out along
5-hole black diagonal edge

Layer 4 (orange lines)
10 holes x 10 holes
Cut 8, cutting out along
3-hole black diagonal edge

Layer 5 (green lines)
8 holes x 8 holes
Cut 8, cutting out upper
right black corner

Layer 6 (red lines)
6 holes x 6 holes
Cut 8

Layer 7 (purple lines)
4 holes x 4 holes
Cut 8

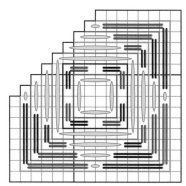

**Stack-n-Stitch Jewel Tone
Top Corner Square B**
Stitch 2

COLOR KEY	
¹/₁₆-Inch Metallic Needlepoint Yarn	**Yards**
☐ Gold #PM51	30
#3 Pearl Cotton	
╱ Ultra dark pistachio green	
#890 Straight Stitch	35
╱ Very dark mauve	
#3685 Straight Stitch	35

Color numbers given are for Rainbow Gallery
Plastic Canvas 10 Metallic Needlepoint Yarn and
DMC #3 pearl cotton.

Floral Surprise

Design by Betty Hansen

Tiny rosebuds and fine baby leaves will wrap your spirit in a wreath of tranquility!

Skill Level: Intermediate

Size: Fits boutique-style tissue box

Materials

- 2 (12-inch x 18-inch) sheets stiff 7-count plastic canvas
- Worsted weight yarn as listed in color key
- #16 tapestry needle
- 1/2-inch plastic ring

Cutting & Stitching

1. Cut plastic canvas according to graphs (pages 112, 113 and 114). Cut one 29-hole x 29-hole piece for lining back and three 29-hole x 37-hole pieces for lining sides and top. All lining pieces and drawer front will remain unstitched.

2. Stitch topper pieces following graphs, working dark country blue Reverse Gobelin Stitches on center motif of topper sides and back before working dark country blue Continental Stitches.

3. Stitch drawer facing, base, back and sides following graphs, leaving orange Whipstitch line on facing unworked at this time.

4. When background stitching is completed, work burgundy and dark green French Knots, wrapping needle two times for burgundy French Knots and one time for green French Knots.

5. Overcast top edge of topper front with white. Overcast around top, sides and bottom edges of drawer facing from dot to dot with dark country blue and off-white, leaving top edges between dots unstitched.

6. Using dark country blue, Overcast inside edges of topper front and top edges of drawer sides and back. Do not Overcast top edge of drawer front.

7. For drawer handle, use burgundy yarn to work a Buttonhole

Stitch (page 113) around 1/2-inch plastic ring, covering completely. Slip a length of yarn through stitching on ring, then thread from front to back through hole indicated on drawer facing; secure ends on backside.

Assembly

1. For lining, use off-white to Whipstitch front and back to sides, then Whipstitch front, back and sides to top.

2. For topper, using dark country blue through step 3, Whipstitch front and back to sides, Whipstitching front to sides from dot to dot. Whipstitch front back, and sides to top.

3. Insert lining in assembled topper, making sure to match front pieces, then Whipstitch bottom edges of lining and topper together. Overcast remaining edges of topper.

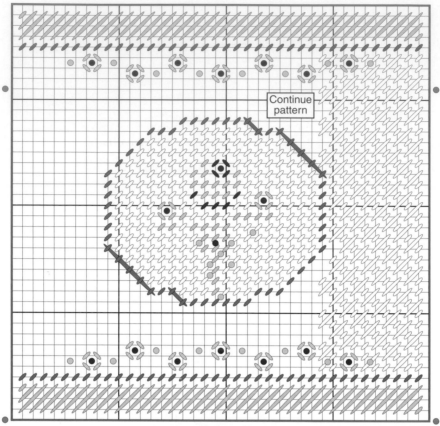

Floral Surprise Topper Side
39 holes x 39 holes
Cut 2

4. Using off-white and with right sides facing, Whipstitch drawer front and back to drawer sides, then Whipstitch front, back and sides to drawer base.

5. Center drawer facing in front of drawer front, then Whipstitch top edges together and work Continental Stitches along orange Whipstitch line with dark country blue.

6. Insert drawer in slot at top. ❖

COLOR KEY	
Worsted Weight Yarn	**Yards**
☐ Off-white	90
☐ Country blue	18
■ Dark country blue	13
☐ Medium green	10
☐ Rose	9
■ Burgundy	9
● Green French Knot	
● Burgundy French Knot	
● Attach handle	

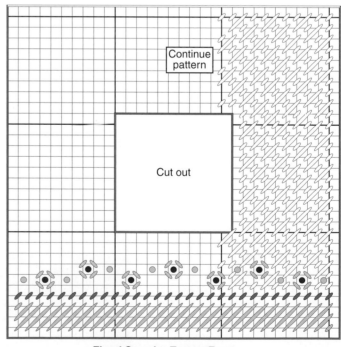

Floral Surprise Topper Front
31 holes x 31 holes
Cut 1

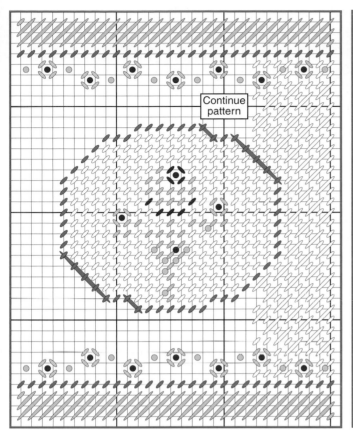

Floral Surprise Topper Back
31 holes x 39 holes
Cut 1

Continue pattern

Floral Surprise Topper Top
31 holes x 39 holes
Cut 1

Continue pattern

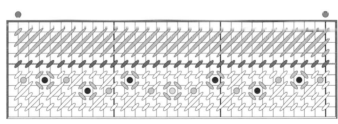

Floral Surprise Drawer Facing
31 holes x 9 holes
Cut 1

Buttonhole Stitch

COLOR KEY	
Worsted Weight Yarn	**Yards**
☐ Off-white	90
▦ Country blue	18
▦ Dark country blue	13
▦ Medium green	10
▦ Rose	9
▪ Burgundy	9
● Green French Knot	
● Burgundy French Knot	
○ Attach handle	

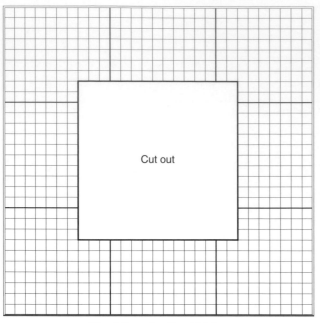

Floral Surprise Front Lining
29 holes x 29 holes
Cut 1
Do not stitch

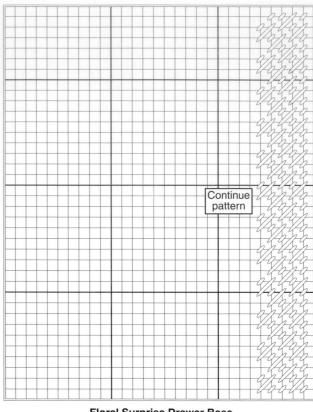

Floral Surprise Drawer Base
29 holes x 37 holes
Cut 1

COLOR KEY	
Worsted Weight Yarn	**Yards**
☐ Off-white	90
▨ Country blue	18
■ Dark country blue	13
▨ Medium green	10
▨ Rose	9
■ Burgundy	9
○ Green French Knot	
● Burgundy French Knot	
○ Attach handle	

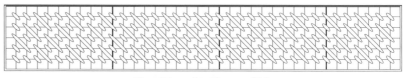

Floral Surprise Drawer Side
37 holes x 6 holes
Cut 2

Floral Surprise Drawer Front & Back
29 holes x 6 holes
Cut 2
Stitch back as graphed
Do not stitch front

Gold Ribbon

Design by Kathy Wirth

Treat yourself like royalty with the richly patterned elegance of this jewel-studded topper!

Skill Level: Intermediate

Size: Fits boutique-style tissue box

Materials

- 1½ sheets 7-count plastic canvas
- Worsted weight yarn as listed in color key
- ⅛-inch-wide Plastic Canvas 7 Metallic Needle-point Yarn by Rainbow Gallery as listed in color key
- #16 tapestry needle
- 4 yards ½-inch-wide metallic gold ribbon
- 12 (12mm) round antique white pearl cabochons #X554-427 from The Beadery
- Hot-glue gun

Project Note

Keep yellow gold metallic needlepoint yarn and ½-inch-wide metallic gold ribbon flat and smooth while stitching.

Instructions

1. Cut and stitch plastic canvas according to graphs (page 116), leaving area at top of topper sides and

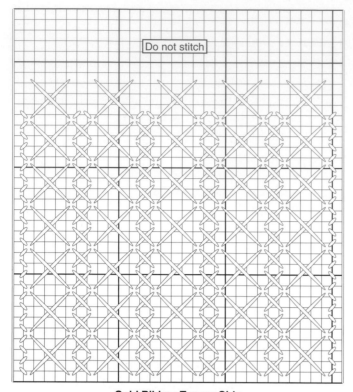

Gold Ribbon Topper Side
31 holes x 35 holes
Cut 4

blue shaded areas unstitched as indicated.

2. Cut 20 (7-inch) lengths $1/2$-inch-wide gold ribbon. Thread five vertical lengths under large Cross Stitches on each topper side. Fold about $1\,1/2$ inches to inside over bottom edge, sliding ribbon under yarn on backside. Glue ribbon ends on front and back to secure.

3. Overcast inside edges of cap top and bottom edges of cap sides with yellow gold metallic needlepoint yarn.

4. Using white and yellow gold, Whipstitch cap sides together. Using white, Whipstitch cap sides to top; Whipstitch topper sides together. Top and bottom edges of topper sides will remain unstitched.

5. Place cap on topper sides; glue to secure. Glue cabochons to cap where indicated in blue shaded areas. ❖

COLOR KEY	
Worsted Weight Yarn	**Yards**
☐ White	55
$1/8$-Inch Metallic Needlepoint Yarn	
☐ Yellow gold #PC7	12
Color number given is for Rainbow Gallery Plastic Canvas 7 Metallic Needlepoint Yarn.	

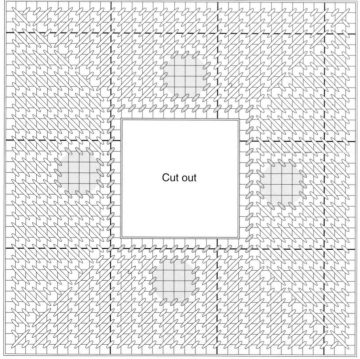

Gold Ribbon Cap Top
33 holes x 33 holes
Cut 1

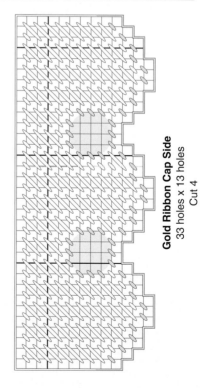

Gold Ribbon Cap Side
33 holes x 13 holes
Cut 4

Country Star Quilt

Design by Angie Arickx

Clever quilt patterning and traditionally popular colors make this topper a natural fit for an elegant bedroom!

Skill Level: Beginner

Size: Fits regular-size tissue box

Materials
- 1¹/₂ sheets 7-count plastic canvas
- Uniek Needloft plastic canvas yarn as listed in color key
- #16 tapestry needle

Instructions

1. Cut plastic canvas according to graphs (pages 118 and 119).

2. Stitch ends following graphs. Stitch sides and top, working left half of each piece as graphed; turn graphs 180 degrees and stitch right halves.

3. Using burgundy throughout, Overcast inside edges of top and bottom edges of sides and ends. Whipstitch sides to ends, then Whipstitch sides and ends to top. ❖

Country Star Quilt End
35 holes x 23 holes
Cut 2

Center Hole

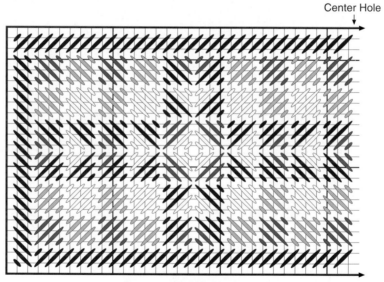

Country Star Quilt Side
65 holes x 23 holes
Cut 2
Stitch left half of each side as graphed
Turn graph 180 degrees and stitch right half

COLOR KEY	
Plastic Canvas Yarn	**Yards**
■ Burgundy #03	52
■ Forest #29	24
□ Eggshell #39	19
▨ Camel #43	23
Color numbers given are for Uniek Needloft plastic canvas yarn.	

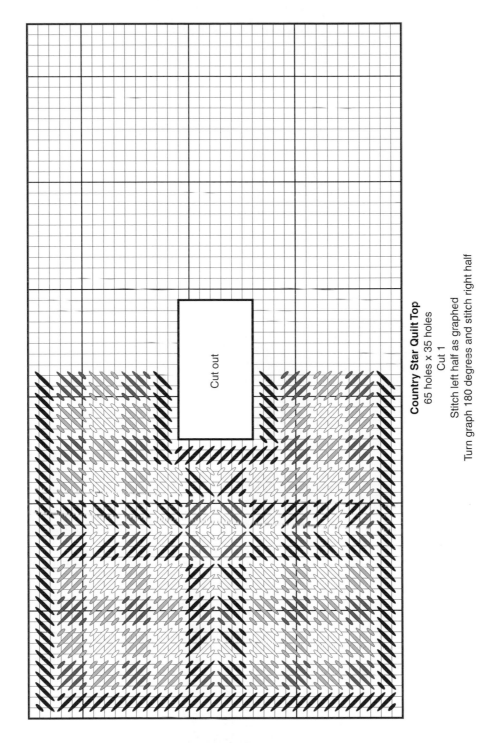

Country Star Quilt Top
65 holes x 35 holes
Cut 1
Stitch left half as graphed
Turn graph 180 degrees and stitch right half

Cut out

COLOR KEY	
Plastic Canvas Yarn	**Yards**
■ Burgundy #03	52
■ Forest #29	24
□ Eggshell #39	19
▨ Camel #43	23
Color numbers given are for Uniek Needloft plastic canvas yarn.	

Red Toile

Design by Cynthia Roberts

Reminiscent of time-treasured redwork, this exquisite topper
sprinkles your room with French-country class!

Skill Level: Beginner

Size: Fits boutique-style tissue box

Materials

• 1¹/₂ sheets 7-count plastic canvas

• Worsted weight yarn as listed in color key

• #16 tapestry needle

Instructions

1. Cut plastic canvas according to graphs.

2. Stitch pieces following graphs, working uncoded areas with off-white Continental Stitches. Work red Backstitches when background stitching is completed.

3. Using off-white throughout, Overcast inside edges of top and bottom edges of sides. Whipstitch sides together, then Whipstitch sides to top. ❖

COLOR KEY	
Worsted Weight Yarn	**Yards**
■ Red	30
Uncoded areas are off-white Continental Stitches	41
╱ Off-white Overcasting and Whipstitching	
╱ Red Backstitch	

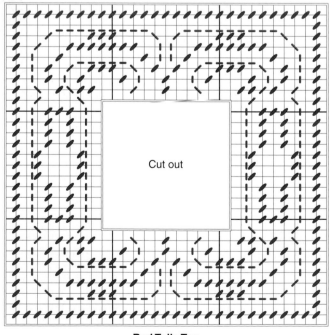

Red Toile Top
30 holes x 30 holes
Cut 1

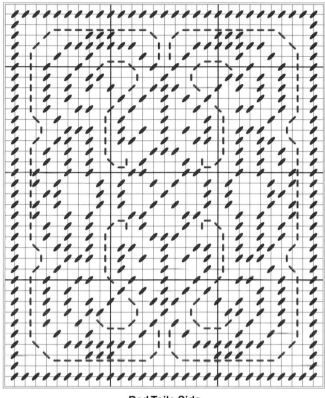

Red Toile Side
30 holes x 36 holes
Cut 4

COLOR KEY

Worsted Weight Yarn	Yards
■ Red	30
Uncoded areas are off-white Continental Stitches	41
⁄ Off-white Overcasting and Whipstitching	
⁄ Red Backstitch	

White Roses on Amethyst
Continued from page 105

COLOR KEY

Plastic Canvas Yarn	Yards
☐ Silver #37	10
☐ Gray #38	5
☐ White #41	12
▨ Lilac #45	21
■ Purple #46	52
Uncoded areas are purple #46 Continental Stitches	

Color numbers given are for Uniek Needloft plastic canvas yarn.

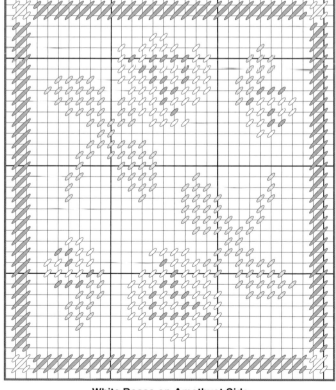

White Roses on Amethyst Side
31 holes x 36 holes
Cut 4

7. Whipstitch organizer sides to organizer front, then Whipstitch sides and front to organizer top. Whipstitch sides and top to side B where indicated with blue lines. Whipstitch unstitched organizer base to front, sides and side B.

8. Whipstitch caddy front and back to sides, then Whipstitch front, back and sides to top. ❖

Cosmetics Caddy Side B
30 holes x 38 holes
Cut 1 from clear

COLOR KEY	
Plastic Canvas Yarn	**Yards**
■ Burgundy #03	20
□ Pink #07	3
▦ Sandstone #16	25
□ Moss #25	6
■ Holly #27	6
□ Flesh tone #56	65
□ Yellow #57	3
Uncoded areas are watermelon	
#55 Continental Stitches	10
╱ Burgundy #03 Backstitch	
○ Yellow #57 French Knot	
Color numbers given are for Uniek Needloft plastic canvas yarn.	

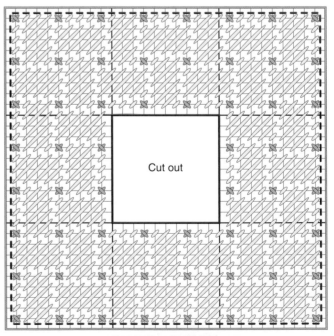

Cosmetics Caddy Top
30 holes x 30 holes
Cut 1 from clear

The Kids' Room

Planning and decorating your children's rooms is a wonderful experience that fills you with memories of your own childhood days! In this chapter we offer a fun-filled selection of bright and cheerful accents designed to complement the delightful exuberance of youth!

Heart Swirls

Design by Kathy Wirth

Curlicue hearts on a background of tumbling squares create
a fun sense of energy and motion for the young girl on the go!

Skill Level: Intermediate

Size: Fits family-size tissue box

Materials

- 2 sheets stiff 7-count plastic canvas
- Coats & Clark Red Heart Classic worsted weight yarn Art. E267 as listed in color key
- Coats & Clark Red Heart Kids worsted weight yarn Art. E711 as listed in color key
- #16 tapestry needle

Instructions

1. Cut plastic canvas according to graphs.

2. Stitch pieces following graphs, working uncoded areas with turquoise Continental Stitches.

3. Overcast inside edges of top and bottom edges of sides and ends with yellow.

4. Using alternating stitches of red and pink, Whipstitch sides to ends, then Whipstitch sides and ends to top. ❖

COLOR KEY	
Worsted Weight Yarn	**Yards**
☐ Yellow #230	11
▨ Amethyst #588	12
■ Red #2390	44
▨ Pink #2734	30
▨ Turquoise #2850	26
Uncoded areas are turquoise	
#2850 Continental Stitches	
Color numbers given are for Coats & Clark Red Heart Classic worsted weight yarn Art. E267 and Kids worsted weight yarn Art. E711.	

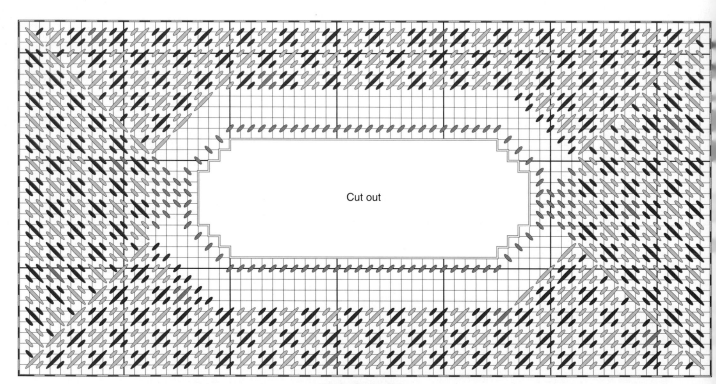

Heart Swirls Top
65 holes x 33 holes
Cut 1

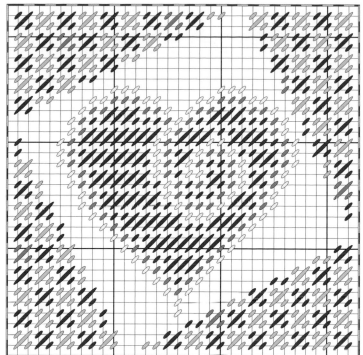

Heart Swirls End
33 holes x 33 holes
Cut 2

COLOR KEY

Worsted Weight Yarn	Yards
☐ Yellow #230	11
■ Amethyst #588	12
■ Red #2390	44
■ Pink #2734	30
■ Turquoise #2850	26

Uncoded areas are turquoise
#2850 Continental Stitches
Color numbers given are for Coats & Clark Red
Heart Classic worsted weight yarn Art. E267
and Kids worsted weight yarn Art. E711.

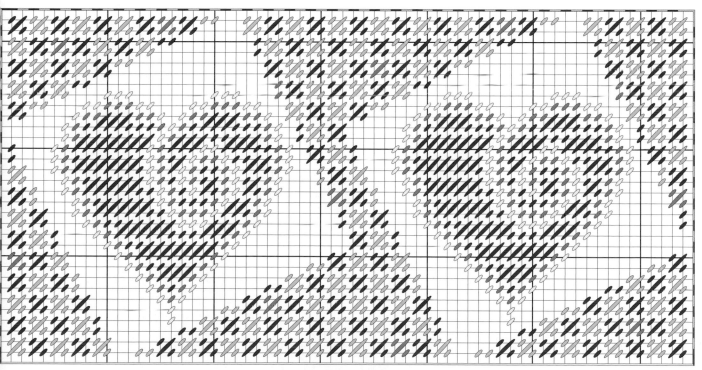

Heart Swirls Side
65 holes x 33 holes
Cut 2

My Favorite Pair of Jeans

Designs by Ronda Bryce

Cleverly stuffed with kid-size treasures, these charming toppers
will soon find a pocket in any child's heart!

Skill Level: Intermediate

Size: Fits boutique-style tissue box

Materials
Each Topper

- 2 sheets 7-count plastic canvas
- Coats & Clark Red Heart Classic worsted weight yarn Art. E267 as listed in color key
- Coats & Clark Red Heart Super Saver worsted weight yarn Art. E300 as listed in color key
- #16 tapestry needle
- 2¹/₂-inch nickel clip-style key chain
- 2 (7mm) nickel jump rings
- Hand-sewing needle
- White sewing thread
- Adhesive to attach studs

Boy Stuff

- 4 (3-inch) Uniek QuickShape plastic canvas radial circles
- Uniek Needloft metallic craft cord as listed in color key
- 2¹/₂ yards ¹/₈-inch-wide brown suede leather lacing
- 2 (³/₄-inch) baseball appliqués
- Bat and baseball appliqué
- 8 (9mm) silver pearl studs
- 6-inch gold decorative chain
- 6mm gold-plated bead
- Gold spacer (approximately 5mm x 8mm)
- ¹/₂-inch pewter star charm

Girl Stuff

- 2 yards ¹/₈-inch-wide brown suede leather lacing

- 2 (4½-inch) squares pink felt
- Large sharp needle
- ½-inch pink ribbon rose
- 1¼-inch light pink ribbon flower
- 2 (⅞-inch) fuchsia daisy appliqués
- 2¼-inch wide pink heart appliqué
- 2½-inch tan miniature bear
- Size 4/0 snap set
- 8 (4mm) gold decorative studs
- ½-inch pewter heart charm
- White paper
- Pink sewing thread

Toppers & Pockets

Cutting & Stitching

1. Cut one top, four sides and four pockets for each topper from plastic canvas according to graphs (pages 129 and 147).

2. Stitch pieces following graphs, working orange Running Stitches when background stitching is completed.

3. Using denim heather throughout, Overcast pockets and inside edges on tops. Overcast bottom edges and inside edges on sides.

Assembly

1. Adhere silver studs to boy's pockets and gold studs to girl's pockets where indicated on graph.

2. For girl stuff, using hand-sewing needle and pink thread, attach one fuchsia daisy each to two pockets and 1¼-inch light pink ribbon flower to a third pocket. Using white thread, attach heart appliqué to corner on one top.

3. For boy stuff, using hand-sewing needle and white thread, attach one baseball appliqué each to two pockets; attach bat and baseball to corner on remaining top.

4. Using denim heather throughout, tack one pocket to each side where indicated with red lines on side graph. Whipstitch corresponding sides together.

5. Cut ½ yard suede leather lacing for each corner. Lace through holes on sides, beginning at top and threading from back to front. Tie tails in a knot at bottom; trim to desired length.

6. Whipstitch tops to corresponding sides with denim heather.

Boy Stuff

Whistle

1. Cut one whistle body from plastic canvas accord-

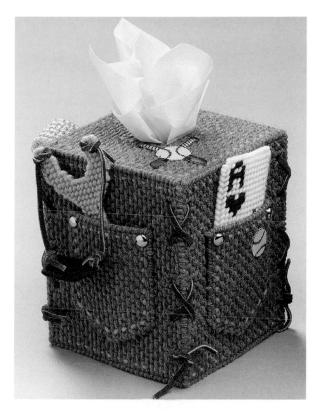

ing to graph (page 128). Cut away and discard five outermost rows of holes from two plastic canvas radial circles for whistle sides.

2. Using white/silver through step 3, stitch body following graph. Continental Stitch each side, working a Cross Stitch in center.

3. Overcast short edges and inside edges of whistle body, then Whipstitch body around edges of sides, Overcasting edges on extended end of body while Whipstitching.

4. Attach jump ring to top edge of whistle where indicated on body graph. Attach remaining jump ring to star charm. Attach both jump rings to key ring, then attach key ring to a top hole on a pocket.

Sling Shot

1. Cut one sling shot and one sling shot strap from plastic canvas according to graphs (page 129).

2. Stitch and Overcast pieces following graphs.

3. Cut two 9-inch lengths of suede leather lacing. Thread one length through each hole on strap and tie in a knot. Tie remaining ends around top of sling shot.

4. Place sling shot in second pocket.

Playing Card

1. Cut one playing card from plastic canvas according to graph (page 147).

2. Stitch and Overcast piece following graph, working uncoded area with white Continental Stitches.

3. Insert card in third pocket.

Pocket Watch

1. Cut one watch face from plastic canvas according to graph (this page). Cut away and discard four outermost rows of holes from remaining two radial circles for watch case.

2. Continental Stitch and Overcast cases with gold, working a Cross Stitch in center.

3. Stitch and Overcast watch face following graph, working uncoded area with white Continental Stitches. Work black Straight Stitches and gold Backstitches on watch face when background stitching is completed.

4. With wrong sides together, center and stitch watch face to one case with hand-sewing needle and white thread.

5. With watch facing up and wrong side of remaining case facing up, tack circles together along three adjacent holes.

6. Using sewing needle and white thread, attach spacer, then gold bead to top of case above watch face.

7. Attach one end of decorative gold chain to hole on case near bead and spacer. Attach other end of chain to top edge of topper above fourth pocket. Place watch in pocket.

Girl Stuff

Diary

1. Cut and stitch one diary from plastic canvas according to graph (page 147); Overcast with grenadine.

2. Using hand-sewing needle and pink thread throughout, attach 1/2-inch pink ribbon rose to right side of strap where indicated on graph. Attach snap to wrong side of strap and to right side of diary where indicated on graph.

3. Cut 10 (1-inch x 2 1/4-inch) pieces from white paper. Place together like pages in a book, then fold in half so they measure 1 inch x 1 1/8 inch.

4. Center paper on wrong side of diary and attach with two petal pink Straight Stitches over fold of papers. Snap diary shut.

5. Attach nickel jump rings to heart charm and edge of diary at

fold, then attach both jump rings to key ring. Attach key ring to a top hole on a pocket.

Hankies & Bear

1. Using large sharp needle, work a Blanket Stitch (this page) around edges of each felt square.

2. Fold hankies and insert into pockets on opposite sides of topper.

3. Place bear in remaining pocket. ❖

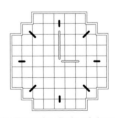

Blanket Stitch

My Favorite Pair of Jeans Watch Face
9 holes x 9 holes
Cut 1

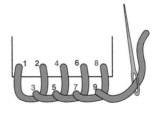

Extended End

My Favorite Pair of Jeans Whistle Body
37 holes x 5 holes
Cut 1

COLOR KEY

Worsted Weight Yarn	Yards
■ Cherry red #319	3
■ Brown #328	3
▢ Linen #330	5
▢ Petal pink #373	4
■ Denim heather #408	90
■ Grenadine #730	7
Uncoded areas are white #311 Continental Stitches	6
⁄ White #311 Overcasting	
⁄ Orange #245 Running Stitch	8
✓ Black #312 Straight Stitch	1
Metallic Craft Cord	
Gold #55001	8
White/silver #55008	4
⁄ Gold #55001 Backstitch	
○ Attach stud	
● Attach jump ring	
● Attach ½-inch ribbon rose	
● Attach snap	

Color numbers given are for Coats & Clark Red Heart Classic worsted weight yarn Art. E267 and Super Saver worsted weight yarn Art. E300 and Uniek Needloft metallic craft cord.

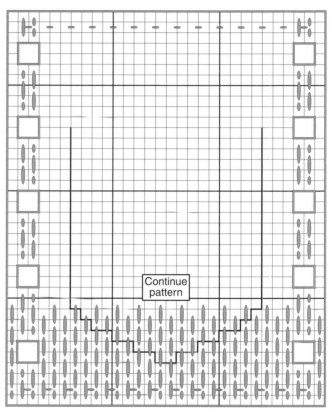

My Favorite Pair of Jeans Side
30 holes x 37 holes
Cut 4 for each topper

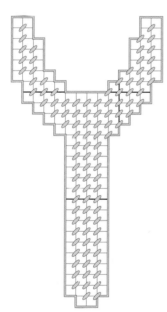

My Favorite Pair of Jeans Sling Shot
14 holes x 27 holes
Cut 1

My Favorite Pair of Jeans Sling Shot Strap
14 holes x 4 holes
Cut 1

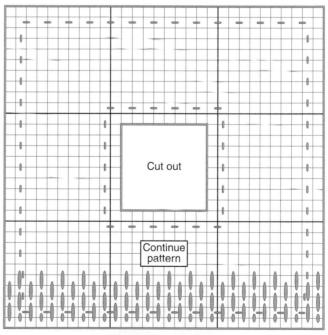

My Favorite Pair of Jeans Top
30 holes x 30 holes
Cut 1 for each topper

Graphs continued on page 147

Just Ducky

Design by Kathy Wirth

Your little sailor will love this seafaring set of darling ducks!

Skill Level: Intermediate

Size: Fits regular-size tissue box

Materials

- 1¹/₂ sheets 10-count plastic canvas
- Coats & Clark Red Heart Classic worsted weight yarn Art. E267 as listed in color key
- Coats & Clark Red Heart Kids worsted weight yarn Art. E711 as listed in color key
- #20 tapestry needle

Project Note

To more easily thread needle, cut ¹/₂-inch square from sticky part of sticky note paper. Fold paper in half over yarn end and insert through needle's eye.

Instructions

1. Cut plastic canvas according to graphs (pages 131 and 132).

2. Stitch pieces following graphs, using 1 strand yarn throughout. Straight Stitch white highlights of ducks' eyes when background stitching is completed.

3. Using blue, Overcast inside edges of top and bottom edges of sides and ends.

4. Using blue, white and turquoise, Whipstitch sides to ends, then Whipstitch sides and ends to top, working Whipstitching so stitches are straight instead of slanted. ❖

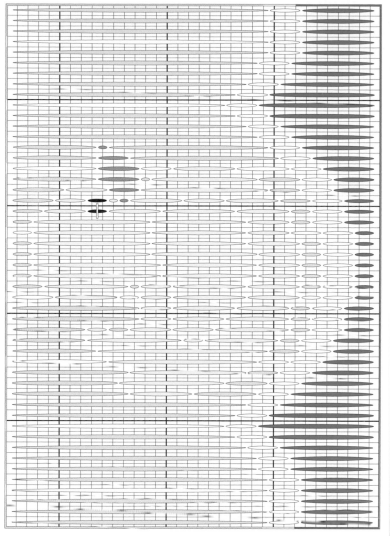

Just Ducky End
49 holes x 35 holes
Cut 2

COLOR KEY

Worsted Weight Yarn	Yards
☐ White #1	19
■ Black #12	1
☐ Yellow #2230	19
▨ Orange #2252	1
■ Blue #2845	35
☐ Turquoise #2850	16
⟋ White #1 Straight Stitch	

Color numbers given are for Coats & Clark Red Heart Classic worsted weight yarn Art. E267 and Kids worsted weight yarn Art. E711

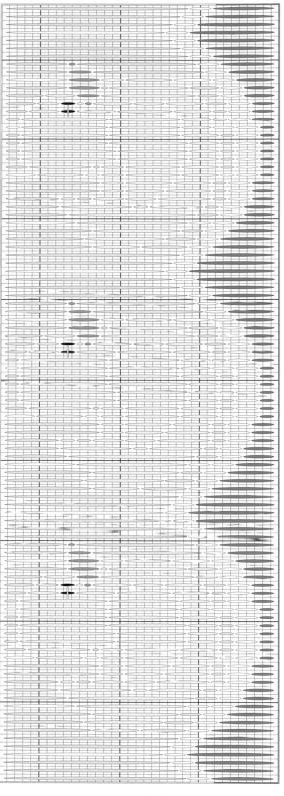

Just Ducky Side
97 holes x 35 holes
Cut 2

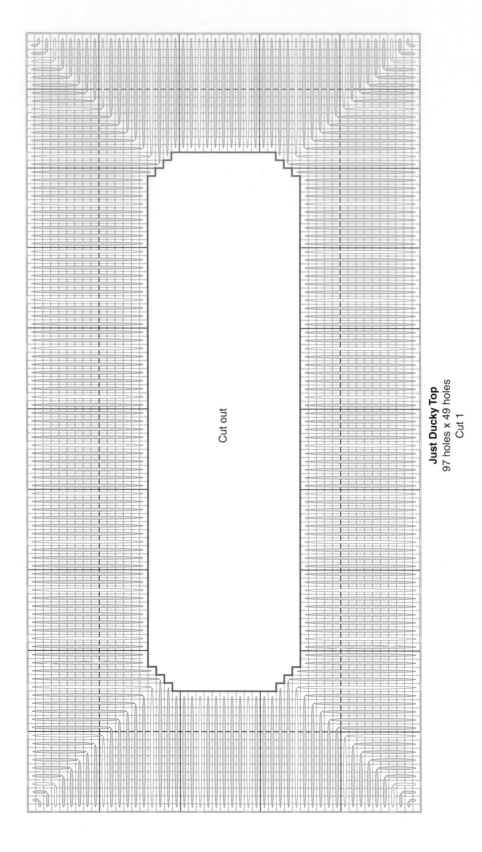

Cut out

Just Ducky Top
97 holes x 49 holes
Cut 1

Happy Faces

Designs by Kimberly A. Suber

This peppy pair of projects will surround your child with a happy horde of smiling faces!

Skill Level: Beginner

Size: Fits boutique-style tissue box

Materials
Each Topper

- 1½ sheets 7-count plastic canvas
- #16 tapestry needle

Topper A

- Coats & Clark Red Heart Kids worsted weight yarn Art. E711 as listed in color key
- Coats & Clark Red Heart Super Saver worsted weight yarn Art. E300 as listed in color key

Topper B

- Coats & Clark Red Heart Classic worsted weight yarn Art. E267 as listed in color key

Instructions

1. Cut plastic canvas according to graphs (page 135).

2. Stitch pieces following graphs, working uncoded areas on topper A with pale plum Continental Stitches and uncoded areas on topper B with tangerine Continental Stitches.

3. When background stitching is completed, work Backstitches and Straight Stitches with 2 plies black.

4. Using full strand black for each topper, Overcast inside edges of top and bottom edges of sides. Whipstitch sides together, then Whipstitch sides to top. ❖

Graphs continued on page 135

Goldfish Bowl

Design by Maryanne Moreck

Your child is sure to get along "swimmingly" with these cheerful freshwater friends!

Skill Level: Beginner

Size: Fits boutique-style tissue box

Materials

- 1½ sheets 7-count plastic canvas
- Worsted weight yarn as listed in color key
- #16 tapestry needle

Instructions

1. Cut plastic canvas according to graphs (this page and page 135).

2. Stitch pieces following graphs, working turquoise Backstitches and black Straight Stitches when background stitching is completed.

3. Using white throughout, Overcast inside edges of top and bottom edges of sides. Whipstitch sides together, then Whipstitch sides to top. ❖

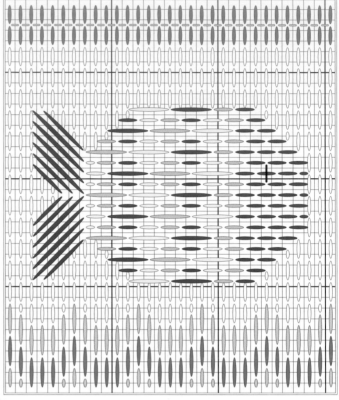

Goldfish Bowl Side
31 holes x 37 holes
Cut 4

COLOR KEY	
Worsted Weight Yarn	**Yards**
☐ White	40
■ Dark turquoise	16
☐ Turquoise	15
■ Bright orange	15
☐ Yellow orange	6
☐ Yellow	6
✎ Turquoise Backstitch	
✦ Black Straight Stitch	1

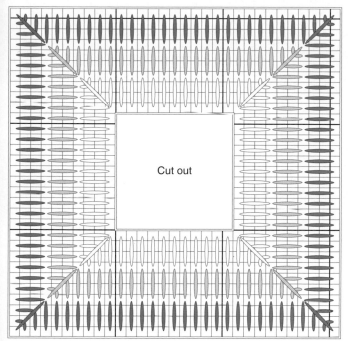

Goldfish Bowl Top
31 holes x 31 holes
Cut 1

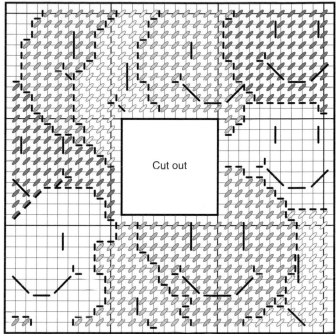

Happy Faces Top
31 holes x 31 holes
Cut 1 for each topper

Happy Faces
Continued from page 133

COLOR KEY	
TOPPER A	
Worsted Weight Yarn	**Yards**
☐ Bright yellow #324	16
☐ Lime #2652	15
☐ Pink #2734	15
☐ Turquoise #2850	15
Uncoded areas are pale plum #579 Continental Stiches	16
✎ Black #312 Backstitch, Straight Stitch Overcasting and Whipstitching	15

Color numbers given are for Coats & Clark Red Heart Kids worsted weight yarn Art. E711 and Super Saver worsted weight yarn Art. E300.

COLOR KEY	
TOPPER B	
Worsted Weight Yarn	**Yards**
☐ Yellow #230	16
☐ Emerald green #676	15
☐ Skipper blue #848	15
☐ Jockey red #902	15
Uncoded areas are tangerine #253 Continental Stiches	16
✎ Black #12 Backstitch, Straight Stitch Overcasting and Whipstitching	15

Color numbers given are for Coats & Clark Red Heart Classic worsted weight yarn Art. E267.

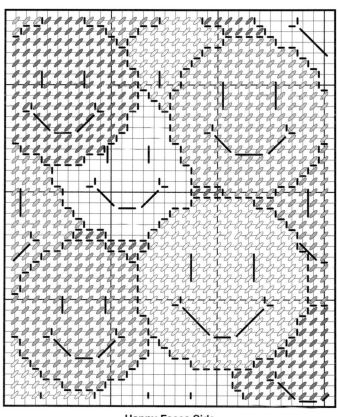

Happy Faces Side
31 holes x 37 holes
Cut 4 for each topper

Baby's Garden

Design by Maryanne Moreck

*Festooned with flowers and loaded with love, this
adorable accent looks right at home in the nursery!*

Skill Level: Intermediate

Size: Fits boutique-style tissue box

Materials
- 2 sheets 7-count plastic canvas
- Worsted weight yarn as listed in color key
- #16 tapestry needle

Instructions

1. Cut plastic canvas according to graphs (pages 137 and 138). Cut two 31-hole x 11-hole pieces for pocket bases. Pocket bases will remain unstitched.

2. Stitch remaining pieces following graphs, working Fern Stitches (page 137) with white and Scotch Stitches with light blue and white.

3. When background stitching is completed, work light blue and pale yellow French Knots.

4. Using white through step 7, Overcast inside edges of top. Whipstitch short sides to long sides from red dot to red dot, then Whipstitch sides to top.

5. Whipstitch side edges of pocket fronts to long sides from black dot to black dot.

6. Whipstitch pocket bases to long sides between brackets and to bottom edges of pocket fronts and topper short sides, Overcasting remaining bottom edges of long sides while Whipstitching.

7. Overcast all remaining edges. ❖

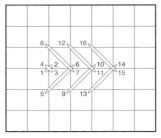

Fern Stitch

COLOR KEY	
Worsted Weight Yarn	**Yards**
□ White	70
▢ Light blue	35
▢ Light green	7
▢ Light rose	5
○ Pale yellow French Knot	2
● Light blue French Knot	

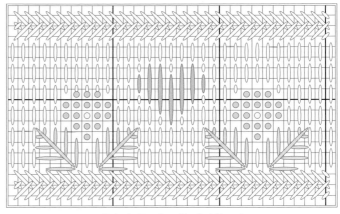

Baby's Garden Pocket Front
31 holes x 19 holes
Cut 2

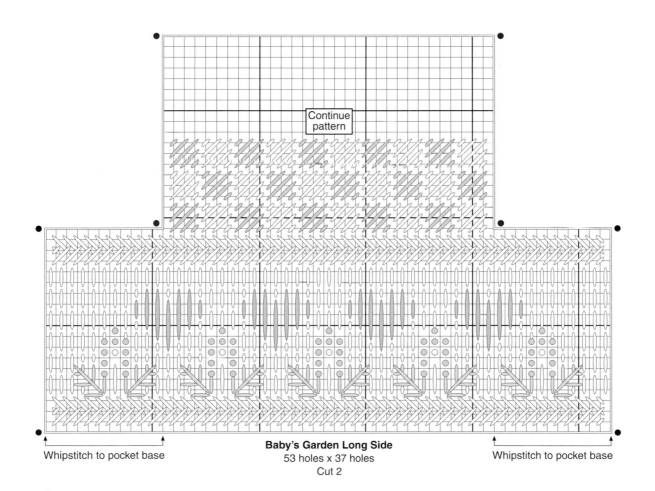

Continue pattern

Whipstitch to pocket base

Whipstitch to pocket base

Baby's Garden Long Side
53 holes x 37 holes
Cut 2

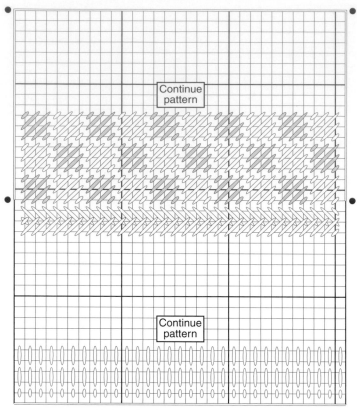

Baby's Garden Topper Short Side
31 holes x 37 holes
Cut 2

COLOR KEY	
Worsted Weight Yarn	**Yards**
☐ White	70
▨ Light blue	35
▨ Light green	7
▨ Light rose	5
○ Pale yellow French Knot	2
● Light blue French Knot	

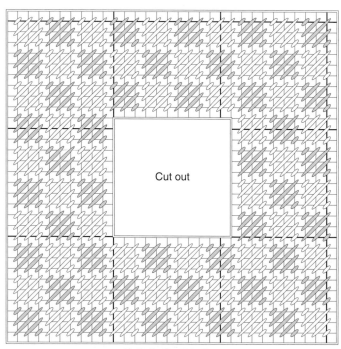

Baby's Garden Top
31 holes x 31 holes
Cut 1

Skateboard Pup

Design by Janelle Giese

Including this spirited skater in your child's room decor is definitely a "cool move!"

Skill Level: Advanced

Size: Fits boutique-style tissue box

Materials
- 1½ sheets 7-count plastic canvas
- Coats & Clark Red Heart Classic worsted weight yarn Art. 267 as listed in color key
- Elmore-Pisgah Inc. Honeysuckle rayon chenille yarn as listed in color key
- Kreinik Heavy (#32) Braid as listed in color key
- Kreinik metallic Cord as listed in color key
- #5 pearl cotton as listed in color key
- #16 tapestry needle

Project Note

The triangle, heart, square, inverted triangle and diamond shapes designate Continental Stitches.

Instructions

1. Cut plastic canvas according to graphs (page 140).

2. Stitch pieces following graphs, working uncoded areas on front with mist green Continental Stitches.

3. When background stitching is completed, use a full strand black yarn to stitch wheels, eyes and nose, passing over nose two times as graphed.

4. Using black pearl cotton, embroider features of pup and skateboard.

5. Work silver heavy (#32) braid embroidery next, working swoosh marks, swirls and the word "YES!" with silver braid as the laid stitches and using silver metallic cord as the couching thread.

6. When silver stitching is completed, stitch next to the braid stitches on the word "YES!" with black pearl cotton.

7. Overcast inside edges of top with peacock green. Using light seafoam throughout, Whipstitch front and back to sides, then Whipstitch front, back and sides to top. Overcast bottom edges. ❖

COLOR KEY

Worsted Weight Yarn	Yards
△ White #1	2
■ Black #12	1
♥ Peacock green #508	18
⬭ Parakeet #513	37
⬭ Light seafoam #683	10
◆ Skipper blue #848	1
▼ Olympic blue #849	1
⬧ Country red #914	2
♥ Cardinal #917	1
Uncoded areas are mist green #681 Continental Stitches	54
⬧ Black #12 Backstitch and Straight Stitch	
Rayon Chenille Yarn	
◇ Honey #7	4
▲ Camel #43	4
Heavy (#32) Braid	
⬭ Silver #001	3
⬭ Silver #001 Straight Stitch and Couching Stitch	
Metallic Cord	
⬭ Silver #001 Couching Stitch	3
#5 Pearl Cotton	
⬧ Black Backstitch and Straight Stitch	6

Color numbers given are for Coats & Clark Red Heart Classic worsted weight yarn Art. E267, Elmore-Pisgah Inc. Honeysuckle rayon chenille yarn, and Kreinik Heavy (#32) Braid and metallic cord.

Skateboard Pup Front
30 holes x 36 holes
Cut 1

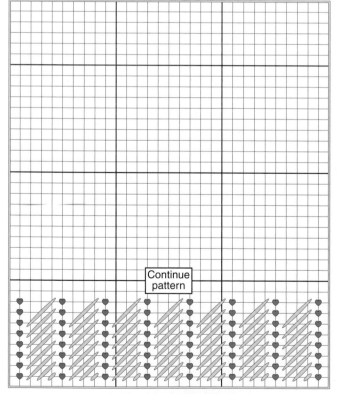

Skateboard Pup Side/Back
30 holes x 36 holes
Cut 3

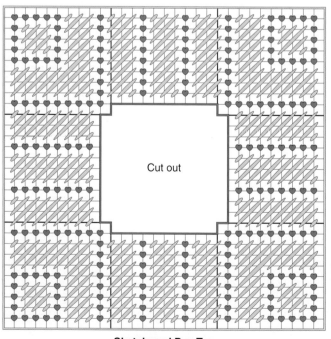

Skateboard Pup Top
30 holes x 30 holes
Cut 1

Tutu Bear

Design by Janelle Giese

Dainty and delicate, this "beary" ballerina will stay on her toes to keep your child happy!

Skill Level: Advanced

Size: Fits boutique-style tissue box

Materials

- 1¹/₂ sheets 7-count plastic canvas
- Coats & Clark Red Heart Classic worsted weight yarn Art. 267 as listed in color key
- Elmore-Pisgah Inc. Honeysuckle rayon chenille yarn as listed in color key
- DMC #3 pearl cotton as listed in color key
- DMC #5 pearl cotton as listed in color key
- #16 tapestry needle
- 20 Mill Hill Products sapphire #80168 medium bugle beads from Gay Bowles Sales Inc.
- Mill Hill Products glass seed beads from Gay Bowles Sales Inc.:
  45 pale peach #00148

155 dusty rose #02005

- 5⁵/₈ yards ¹/₈-inch-wide dark pink ribbon to match pale rose yarn
- 2¹/₄ yards ¹/₈-inch-wide light pink ribbon to match lily pink yarn
- 4 yards bead thread
- Beading needle
- Thick white glue

Cutting & Stitching

1. Cut plastic canvas according to graphs (page 143).

2. Stitch pieces following graphs, working uncoded

area on front with off-white Continental Stitches. Do not work Turkey Loop Stitches at this time.

3. Overcast inside edges on top and bottom edges of front, back and sides with off-white.

4. When background stitching is completed, using black brown pearl cotton throughout, work Cross Stitch for nose, passing over each stitch three times. Work French Knot eyes, wrapping needle three times; work ears and mouth.

5. Using 1 ply off-white yarn, Straight Stitch eye and nose highlights, bringing needle up outside stitch, then piercing center of Cross Stitch and French Knots.

6. Outline bear with dark beige brown. Using medium forest green, Backstitch vine of wreath, then work leaves on vine and in corner motifs of both front and top with two stitches each. Use 2 plies blue jewel to work French Knots on wreath, wrapping each knot one time. Use 2 plies pale rose to work lacing of ballet slipper.

7. Using beading needle and thread, attach beads were indicated on graph. Clusters of three beads are worked with one stitch.

8. Using lily pink and pale rose, work Turkey Loop Stitches where indicated, making loops approximately $3/8$-inch high. Trim loops and fluff, using end of tapestry needle.

Finishing

1. Cut dark pink ribbon as follows: seven 10-inch lengths, nine 12-inch lengths and one 24-inch length.

2. Cut light pink ribbon as follows: one 8-inch length and seven 10-inch lengths.

3. Thread one 12-inch length dark pink ribbon under large Cross Stitches on sides and back where indicated on graph (three ribbons for each side and back). Begin by drawing ends under center Cross Stitch of each row and pulling to edges. Pull on ribbon with fingers to work out twists while threading under stitches.

4. When ribbon lengths are in place, twist end and draw to backside at blue hearts. Twisting ribbon at end of each row will make it narrow enough to make ribbon lines appear straighter, omitting an upward curve at row ends caused by ribbon width.

5. Thread 24-inch length dark pink ribbon where indicated through border on top, drawing to back-side at corners and back up at adjacent corner. Twist at beginning and end of each row as in step 4. Finish by drawing ends through holes to backside at one corner.

6. For bow at top of slipper laces, thread 8-inch length light pink ribbon from back to front through holes indicated with pink hearts. Tie in a bow on front; add dab of glue to secure.

7. Using off-white yarn, Whipstitch front and back to sides, then Whipstitch front, back and sides to top.

8. Place 10-inch lengths of ribbon in seven pairs, each having one light pink and one dark pink length. Tie each pair in a bow; trim ends. Glue to assembled topper where indicated with green triangles. ❖

COLOR KEY	
Worsted Weight Yarn	Yards
☐ Off-white #3	77
■ Light lavender #579	8
☐ Lily pink #719	8
■ Pale rose #755	4
☐ Blue jewel #818	5
Uncoded area on front is off-white #3 Continental Stitches	
⁄ Off-white #3 (1-ply) Straight Stitch	
⁄ Pale rose #755 (2-ply) Straight Stitch	
– Lily pink #719 Turkey Loop Stitch	
– Pale rose #755 Turkey Loop Stitch	
○ Blue jewel #818 (2-ply) French Knot	
Rayon Chenille Yarn	
☐ Beige #4	9
#3 Pearl Cotton	
⁄ Medium forest green #988 Backstitch and Straight Stitch	2
#5 Pearl Cotton	
⁄ Dark beige brown #839 Backstitch and Straight Stitch	3
⁄ Black brown #3371 Backstitch and Cross Stitch	1
⁄ Attach sapphire bugle bead	
○ Attach 1 dusty rose bead	
● Attach 3-bead cluster dusty rose beads	
● Attach 3-bead cluster pale peach beads	
♡ Attach pale pink ribbon bow	
♥ Attach dark pink ribbon	
▲ Attach double ribbon bow	
Color numbers given are for Coats & Clark Red Heart Classic worsted wieght yarn Art. E267, Elmore-Pisgah Honeysuckle rayon chenille yarn and DMC #3 and #5 pearl cotton.	

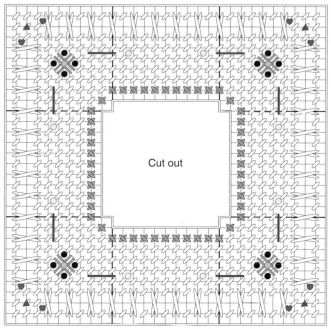

Tutu Bear Top
30 holes x 30 holes
Cut 1

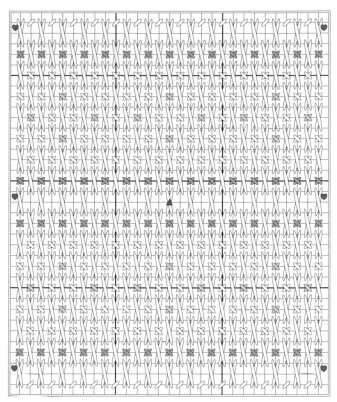

Tutu Bear Side/Back
30 holes x 36 holes
Cut 3

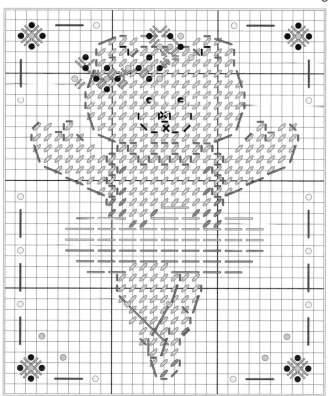

Tutu Bear Side Front
30 holes x 36 holes
Cut 1

Pretty in Pink Kitty

Design by Debra Arch

Your child's room is sure to be the "cat's meow" when you decorate with this fun-loving topper!

Skill Level: Intermediate

Size: Fits boutique-style tissue box

Materials

- 1 artist-size sheet 7-count plastic canvas
- 4-inch square white 7-count plastic canvas
- 2 (6-inch) Uniek QuickShape plastic canvas hearts
- 2 (6-inch) Uniek QuickShape plastic canvas radial circles
- Coats & Clark Red Heart Super Saver worsted weight yarn Art. E300 as listed in color key
- #16 tapestry needle
- 3 yards 1½-inch-wide pink and white minicheck wired-edge ribbon
- 2 (¾-inch) black ball-shaped or dome buttons
- Hot-glue gun

Project Note

When stitching body, body back, top, tail pieces and paws on legs, use 2 strands yarn. Use 1 strand yarn when stitching ear pieces, legs and nose.

Cutting & Stitching

1. Cut body, body back, top, nose, and ear front and back pieces from clear plastic canvas according to graphs (pages 145 and 146).

2. Cut legs from plastic canvas hearts and tail pieces from plastic canvas radial circles according to graphs (pages 146 and 147), cutting away pale peach areas.

3. Cut three strips on the diagonal from white plastic canvas to form "zigzag" whiskers. Trim to about 3 inches long. Set aside.

4. Stitch pieces following graphs and project note, reversing one tail before stitching.

5. Using pink, Overcast nose and bottom edge of ear fronts. Using light gray, Overcast inside edges of top; Overcast bottom edges of body and body back.

Assembly

1. Whipstitch wrong sides of tail pieces together with white and light gray, leaving bottom edges unworked. Whipstitch wrong sides of legs together with white and light gray.

2. For each ear, align points A, B and C on one front to one back, then Whipstitch together with light gray; Overcast remaining edges of ear back.

3. Using light gray throughout, Whipstitch side edges of body to side edges of body back. Whipstitch top to body and body back, Whipstitching bottom edge of tail along back edge through all thicknesses where indicated on top graph.

4. Using photo as a guide, glue button eyes, whiskers, nose, ears and legs in place.

5. Beginning under legs, wrap ribbon up and around back just under top edge, ending under legs other side; glue in place.

6. Make a 4¹/₂-inch-wide six-loop bow from ribbon; glue to top of legs. Make a 2¹/₄-inch-wide two-loop bow from ribbon and glue to base of tail on back.

7. For hair tuft, wrap one strand light gray yarn five times around three fingers. Remove from fingers and tie in center. Glue to top in front of ears. ❖

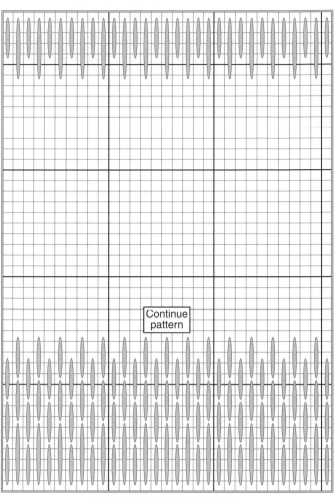

Pretty in Pink Kitty Body Back
31 holes x 45 holes
Cut 1

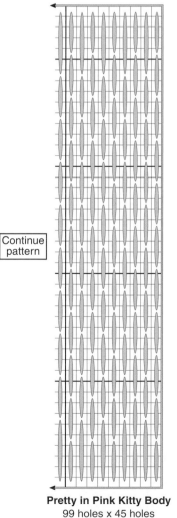

Continue pattern

Pretty in Pink Kitty Body
99 holes x 45 holes
Cut 1

A
B
C

Pretty in Pink Kitty Ear Front
11 holes x 11 holes
Cut 2

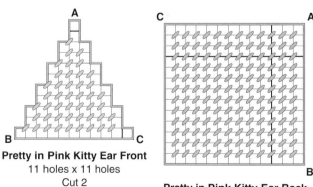

C   A

B

Pretty in Pink Kitty Ear Back
13 holes x 13 holes
Cut 2

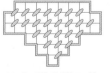

Pretty in Pink Kitty Nose
9 holes x 6 holes
Cut 1

COLOR KEY	
Worsted Weight Yarn	**Yards**
☐ White #311	7
▨ Light gray #341	180
▨ Petal pink #373	7
Color numbers given are for Coats & Clark Red Heart Super Saver worsted weight yarn Art. E300.	

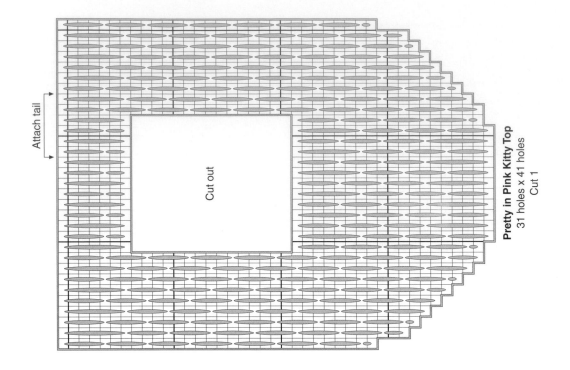

Pretty in Pink Kitty Top
31 holes x 41 holes
Cut 1

Attach tail

Cut out

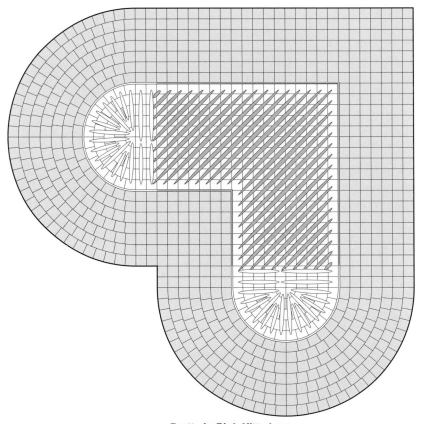

COLOR KEY

Worsted Weight Yarn	Yards
☐ White #311	7
▨ Light gray #341	180
▨ Petal pink #373	7

Color numbers given are for Coats & Clark Red Heart Super Saver worsted weight yarn Art. E300.

Pretty in Pink Kitty Legs
Cut 2 from hearts,
cutting away pale peach area

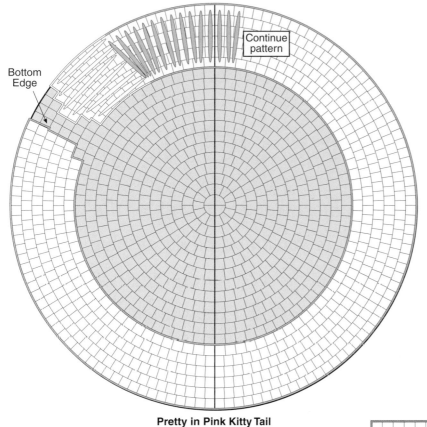

Pretty in Pink Kitty Tail
Cut 2, reverse 1, from radial circles,
cutting away pale peach area

COLOR KEY

Worsted Weight Yarn	Yards
☐ White #311	7
■ Light gray #341	180
☐ Petal pink #373	7

Color numbers given are for Coats &
Clark Red Heart Super Saver worsted
weight yarn Art. E300.

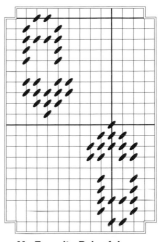

**My Favorite Pair of Jeans
Playing Card**
14 holes x 21 holes
Cut 1

My Favorite Pair of Jeans

Continued from page 129

COLOR KEY

Worsted Weight Yarn	Yards
■ Cherry red #319	3
■ Brown #328	3
☐ Linen #330	5
☐ Petal pink #373	4
■ Denim heather #408	90
■ Grenadine #730	7
Uncoded areas are white #311 Continental Stitches	6
⁄ White #311 Overcasting	
⁄ Orange #245 Running Stitch	8
✓ Black #312 Straight Stitch	1
Metallic Craft Cord	
Gold #55001	8
White/silver #55008	4
⁄ Gold #55001 Backstitch	
○ Attach stud	
● Attach jump ring	
● Attach ½-inch ribbon rose	
● Attach snap	

Color numbers given are for Coats & Clark Red
Heart Classic worsted weight yarn Art. E267 and
Super Saver worsted weight yarn Art. E300 and
Uniek Needloft metallic craft cord.

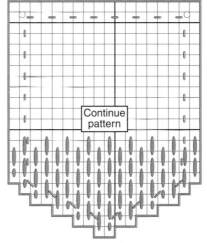

My Favorite Pair of Jeans Pocket
18 holes x 22 holes
Cut 4 for each topper

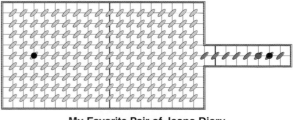

My Favorite Pair of Jeans Diary
27 holes x 10 holes
Cut 1

The Christmas Collection

The holiday season is the most wonderful time of the year for creative decorating! Here you'll find plenty of new and innovative Christmas projects to accentuate any holiday mood, from childlike excitement to exquisite elegance!

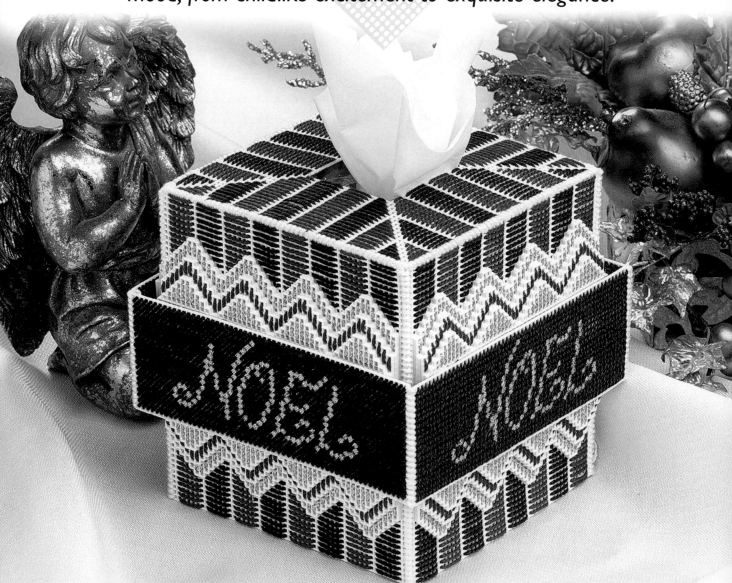

Noel

Design by Kathy Wirth

With the look and feel of an antique Christmas card, this handsome topper says "Season's Greetings" with stunning style!

Skill Level: Intermediate

Size: Fits boutique-style tissue box

Materials
- 4 sheets white 10-count plastic canvas
- DMC #3 pearl cotton as listed in color key
- Kreinik 1/8-inch Ribbon as listed in color key
- Kreinik 1/16-inch Ribbon as listed in color key
- #22 tapestry needle
- #24 tapestry needle
- Hot-glue gun

Project Notes

Use #22 tapestry needle with pearl cotton and 1/8-inch ribbon; use #24 tapestry needle with 1/16-inch ribbon.

Keep ribbon flat and smooth while stitching.

When adding layers, always make sure canvas holes are properly aligned.

Instructions

1. Cut top, sides and noel plaques from plastic canvas according to graphs (this page and pages 150, 151 and 152).

2. Cut layers from plastic canvas as follows: layer A, eight 48-hole x 43-hole pieces along red lines; layer B, eight 48-hole x 37-hole pieces along green lines and red vertical side edges between green lines; layer

C, eight 48-hole x 31-hole pieces along blue lines and red vertical side edges between blue lines.

3. Stitch top, sides and plaques following graphs, working uncoded areas on plaques with medium garnet Continental Stitches. Leave all uncoded areas on top and sides unworked.

4. Place two layer A pieces on one side, aligning edges of layer with red lines on side. Work 1/16-inch Aztec gold ribbon stitches of layer A through all thicknesses.

5. Center two layer B pieces over layer A, aligning top and bottom edges of layer B with green lines. Work bright red pearl cotton stitches of layer B through all thicknesses.

6. Center two layer C pieces over layer B, aligning top and bottom edges of layer C with blue lines.

COLOR KEY	
#3 Pearl Cotton	**Yards**
■ Bright red #666	30
■ Medium garnet #815	66
Uncoded areas on plaque are medium garnet #815 Continental Stitches	
⁄ White Whipstitching	14
1/8-Inch Ribbon	
▨ Aztec gold hi lustre #202HL	8
1/16-Inch Ribbon	
▢ Aztec gold hi lustre #202HL	19
Color numbers given are for DMC #3 pearl cotton and Kreinik 1/8-Inch Ribbon and 1/16-Inch Ribbon.	

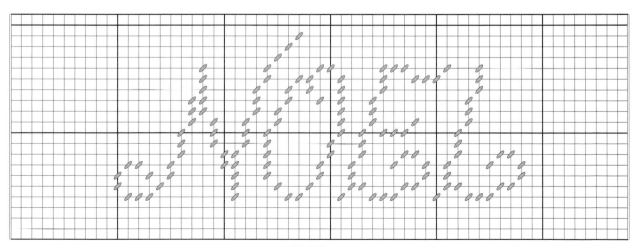

Noel Plaque
58 holes x 21 holes
Cut 4

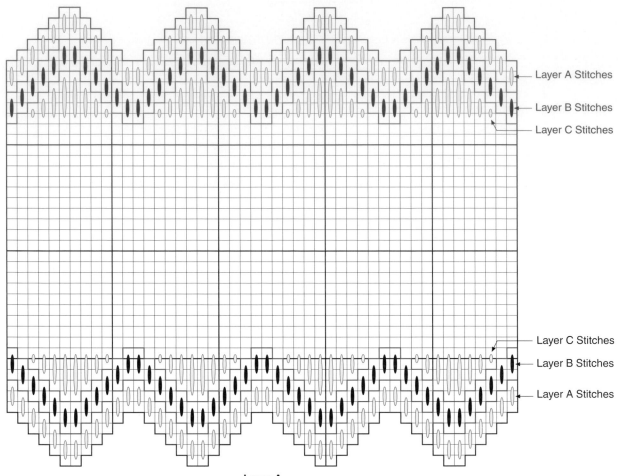

Layer A Stitches

Layer B Stitches

Layer C Stitches

Layer C Stitches

Layer B Stitches

Layer A Stitches

Layer A
48 holes x 43 holes
Cut 8 along red lines

Layer B
48 holes x 37 holes
Cut 8 along green lines and red
vertical side edges between green lines

Layer C
48 holes x 31 holes
Cut 8 along blue lines and red
vertical side edges between blue lines

Work ¹/₁₆-inch Aztec gold ribbon stitches of layer C through all thicknesses. Complete remaining sides following steps 4 through 6.

7. Using white pearl cotton through step 8, Whipstitch sides together then Whipstitch sides to top. Inside edges of top and bottom edges of sides will remain unstitched.

8. Whipstitch side edges of noel plaques together, leaving top and bottom edges unworked.

9. Slide assembled plaques over topper, covering unstitched area at center of layers; glue in place. ❖

COLOR KEY	
#3 Pearl Cotton	**Yards**
■ Bright red #666	30
■ Medium garnet #815	66
Uncoded areas on plaque are medium garnet #815 Continental Stitches	
⁄ White Whipstitching	14
¹/₈-Inch Ribbon	
▨ Aztec gold hi lustre #202HL	8
¹/₁₆-Inch Ribbon	
☐ Aztec gold hi lustre #202HL	19
Color numbers given are for DMC #3 pearl cotton and Kreinik ¹/₈-Inch Ribbon and ¹/₁₆-Inch Ribbon.	

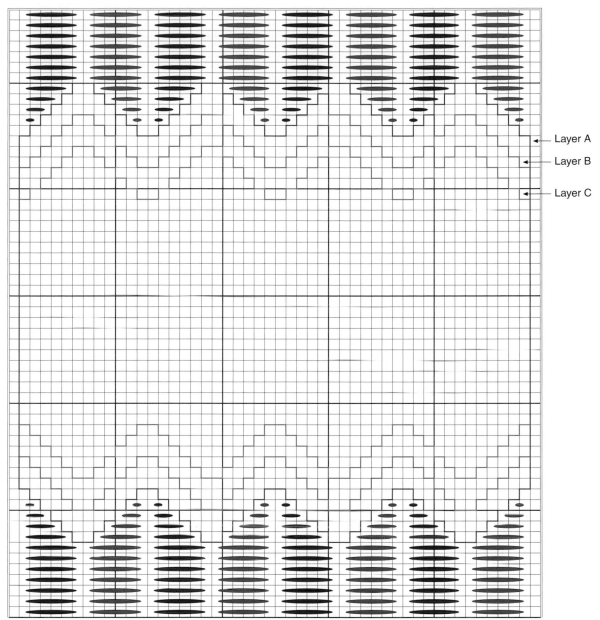

Noel Side
50 holes x 57 holes
Cut 4

COLOR KEY	
#3 Pearl Cotton	**Yards**
■ Bright red #666	30
■ Medium garnet #815	66
Uncoded areas on plaque are medium garnet #815 Continental Stitches	
▱ White Whipstitching	14
¹/₈-Inch Ribbon	
▨ Aztec gold hi lustre #202HL	8
¹/₁₆-Inch Ribbon	
▢ Aztec gold hi lustre #202HL	19
Color numbers given are for DMC #3 pearl cotton and Kreinik ¹/₈-Inch Ribbon and ¹/₁₆-Inch Ribbon.	

Layer A
Layer B
Layer C

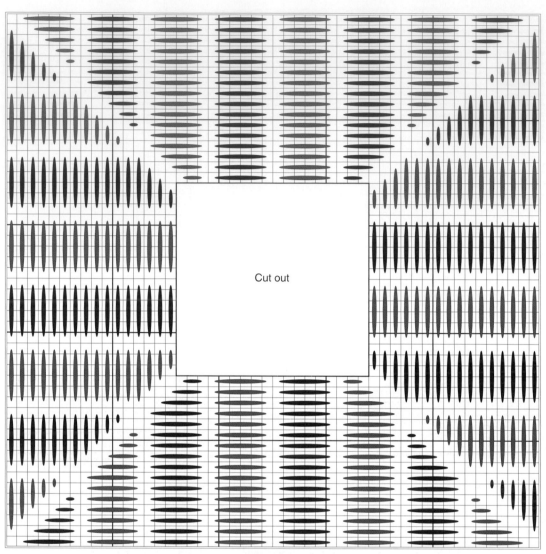

Noel Top
50 holes x 57 holes
Cut 1

COLOR KEY	
#3 Pearl Cotton	**Yards**
■ Bright red #666	30
■ Medium garnet #815	66
Uncoded areas on plaque are medium garnet #815 Continental Stitches	
⁄ White Whipstitching	14
¹⁄₈-Inch Ribbon	
▨ Aztec gold hi lustre #202HL	8
¹⁄₁₆-Inch Ribbon	
☐ Aztec gold hi lustre #202HL	19
Color numbers given are for DMC #3 pearl cotton and Kreinik ¹⁄₈-Inch Ribbon and ¹⁄₁₆-Inch Ribbon.	

Christmas Sophistication

Design by Maryanne Moreck

This stately showpiece has a regal flair that makes it a must for elegant entertaining!

Skill Level: Beginner

Size: Fits boutique-style tissue box

Materials

- 1¹/₂ sheets 7-count plastic canvas
- Worsted weight yarn as listed in color key
- ¹/₈-inch-wide Plastic Canvas 7 Metallic Needlepoint Yarn by Rainbow Gallery as listed in color key
- #16 tapestry needle
- 188 (4mm) gold beads
- Beading needle
- Transparent thread

Instructions

1. Cut plastic canvas according to graphs (this page and page 155).

2. Stitch pieces following graphs, working two Straight Stitches per hole where indicated.

3. Using beading needle and transparent thread, attach beads where indicated.

4. Using dark green throughout, Overcast inside edges of top and bottom edges of sides. Whipstitch sides together, then Whipstitch sides to top. ❖

Graphs continued on page 155

COLOR KEY	
Worsted Weight Yarn	**Yards**
■ Dark green	100
■ Red	40
╱ Dark green Straight Stitch	
╱ Red Straight Stitch	
¹/₈-Inch Metallic Needlepoint Yarn	
☐ Gold #PC1	34
● Attach gold bead	
Color number given is for Rainbow Gallery Plastic Canvas 7 Metallic Needlepoint Yarn.	

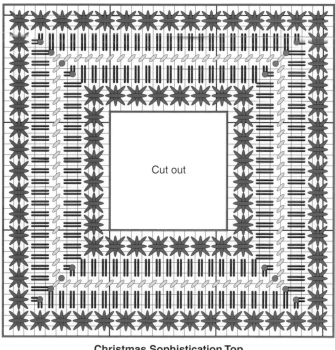

Christmas Sophistication Top
31 holes x 31 holes
Cut 1

Fantasy Tree

Design by Mary T. Cosgrove

You're sure to be in a festive mood when you deck the halls with this magically merry topper!

Skill Level: Intermediate

Size: Fits boutique-style tissue box

Materials

- 2 sheets 7-count plastic canvas
- Uniek Needloft plastic canvas yarn as listed in color key
- Kreinik Heavy (#32) Braid as listed in color key
- #16 tapestry needle
- 7 yards 4mm Madeira Carat kelly green #9724-458 knitted ribbon braid
- 8 (6-inch) lengths green craft wire
- 25 (1/2-inch) gold spoke sequins
- Fabric glue

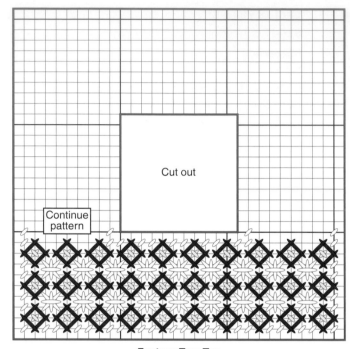

Fantasy Tree Top
31 holes x 31 holes
Cut 1

Topper

1. Cut plastic canvas according to graphs.

2. Stitch pieces following graphs, working Christmas red stitches following Fig. 1 so stitches will be overlapped in a consistent way.

3. Using holly throughout, Overcast inside edges of top and bottom edges of sides. Whipstitch sides together, then Whipstitch sides to top.

Christmas Trees

1. Cut four each of the following lengths from kelly green knitted ribbon braid: 12-inch, 11-inch, 10-inch, 9-inch, 8-inch, 7-inch and 6-inch.

2. Tie each 12-inch length in a bow, leaving 3/4-inch tails. Glue center of bows to sides where indicated at bottom green dot. Tie each 11-inch length in a bow, leaving only a small amount for tails.

3. Repeat with 10-inch, 9-inch, 8-inch and 7-inch lengths, gluing each successively smaller bow at the next green dot up from the bow below it.

4. For each 6-inch length, hold ends together and tie a knot at the bottom, making a loop 1 1/8-inches to

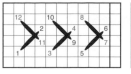
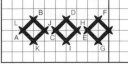

A   **B**

Fig. 1

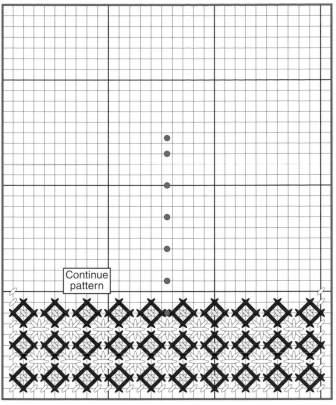

COLOR KEY

Plastic Canvas Yarn	Yards
■ Christmas red #02	65
☐ White #41	52
■ Holly #27 Overcasting and Whipstitching	6
Heavy (#32) Braid	
☐ Gold hi lustre #002HL	19
● Attach knitted ribbon braid	

Color numbers given are for Uniek Needloft plastic canvas yarn and Kreinik Heavy (#32) Braid.

1¹⁄₄-inches long. Glue knots of these loops to the top green dot on sides for top of trees.

5. For gold garland on each tree, wind end of one length of wire around #16 tapestry needle several times to form a small coil. Thread on one gold spoke sequin, then wrap wire around needle in front of gold sequin.

6. Leave about ¹⁄₂ inch of straight craft wire, add a sequin and coil wire in front of it. Repeat adding two more sequins, making a small coil in front of and behind fourth sequin.

7. Repeat with second length, threading on three sequins and making length between sequins a little longer.

8. Using photo as a guide, glue 3-sequin garland to tree above 4-sequin garland.

9. Bring ends of bows forward to give dimension to trees. ❖

Christmas Sophistication
Continued from page 153

COLOR KEY

Worsted Weight Yarn	Yards
■ Dark green	100
■ Red	40
╱ Dark green Straight Stitch	
╱ Red Straight Stitch	
¹⁄₈-Inch Metallic Needlepoint Yarn	
☐ Gold #PC1	34
● Attach gold bead	

Color number given is for Rainbow Gallery Plastic Canvas 7 Metallic Needlepoint Yarn.

Continue pattern

Fantasy Tree Side
31 holes x 37 holes
Cut 4

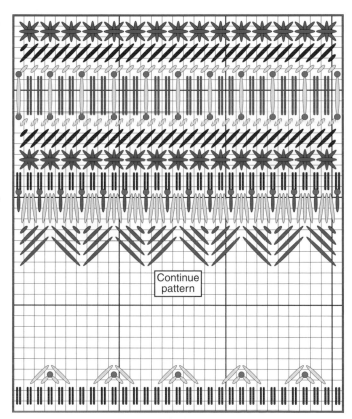

Continue pattern

Christmas Sophistication Side
31 holes x 37 holes
Cut 4

Holiday Wonderland

Design by Kathy Wirth

*Bright red berries and softly falling snow highlight
the seasonal splendor of this fanciful Christmas forest!*

Skill Level: Beginner

Size: Fits boutique-style tissue box

Materials

- 1½ sheets 7-count plastic canvas
- Coats & Clark Red Heart Classic worsted weight yarn Art. E267 as listed in color key
- ⅛-inch-wide Rainbow Gallery Plastic Canvas 7 Metallic Needlepoint Yarn as listed in color key
- #16 tapestry needle
- 36 (9mm) round ruby acrylic faceted stones X613-017 from The Beadery
- 4 (22mm) ruby acrylic faceted stars
- Jewel glue

Instructions

1. Cut plastic canvas according to graphs.

2. Stitch pieces following graphs, working uncoded background around trees on sides with mist green Continental Stitches. Do not stitch uncoded areas on trees shaded with red.

3. When background stitching is completed, work Running Stitches on corners with red metallic needlepoint yarn.

4. Using white throughout, Whipstitch sides to corners, beginning at bottom and working up, easing to fit at top. Overcast top and bottom edges.

5. Glue 9mm round ruby stones to unworked areas on trees shaded with red. Glue acrylic stars to sides at tops of trees. ❖

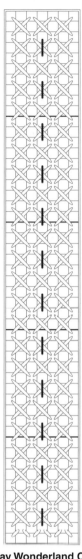

Holiday Wonderland Side
27 holes x 46 holes
Cut 4

Holiday Wonderland Corner
7 holes x 50 holes
Cut 4

COLOR KEY	
Worsted Weight Yarn	**Yards**
☐ White #1	36
☐ Emerald green #676	15
■ Forest green #689	15
Uncoded areas with white background on sides are mist green #681 Continental Stitches	34
✏ Forest green #689 Straight Stitch	
¹/₈-Inch Metallic Needlepoint Yarn	
☐ Silver #PC2	10
✏ Red #PC5 Running Stitch	5
Color numbers given are for Coats & Clark Red Heart Classic worsted weight yarn Art. E267 and Rainbow Gallery Plastic Canvas 7 Metallic Needlepoint Yarn.	

Poinsettia Patchwork

Design by Angie Arickx

*This holiday topper has a radiant warmth and fireside glow
that will keep your thoughts tuned to hearth and home!*

Skill Level: Beginner

Size: Fits regular-size tissue box

Materials

- 1½ sheets 7-count plastic canvas
- Uniek Needloft plastic canvas yarn as listed in color key
- #16 tapestry needle

Instructions

1. Cut plastic canvas according to graphs.

2. Stitch pieces following graphs, stitching right half of top and each side as graphed; turn pieces 180 degrees and stitch remaining halves.

Poinsettia Patchwork End
35 holes x 23 holes
Cut 2

3. Using Christmas red throughout, Overcast inside edges of top and bottom edges of sides and ends. Whipstitch sides to ends, then Whipstitch sides and ends to top. ❖

COLOR KEY	
Plastic Canvas Yarn	**Yards**
■ Black #00	41
■ Red #01	33
■ Christmas red #02	23
■ Christmas green #28	12
☐ Yellow #57	4
Color numbers given are for Uniek Needloft plastic canvas yarn.	

Poinsettia Patchwork Side
65 holes x 23 holes
Cut 2
Stitch right half of each side as graphed,
turn 180 degrees and stitch remaining half

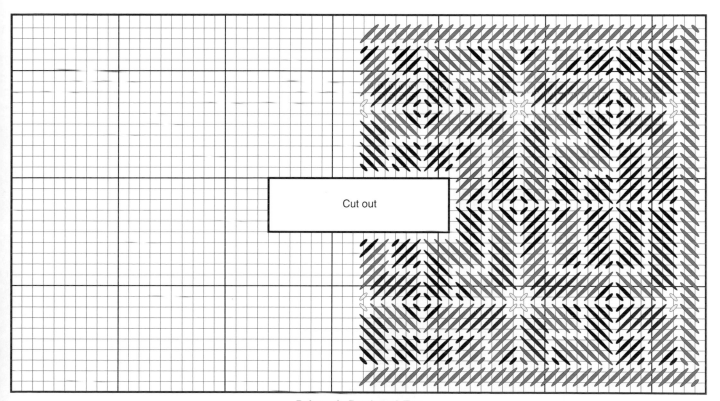

Poinsettia Patchwork Top
65 holes x 35 holes
Cut 1
Stitch right half as graphed,
turn 180 degrees and stitch remaining half

Pink Poinsettia Elegance

Design by Susan Leinberger

*With its nontraditional colors and elegant beaded design,
this majestic topper is sure to be a holiday centerpiece!*

Skill Level: Beginner

Size: Fits boutique-style tissue box

Materials

- 2 sheets 7-count plastic canvas
- 5-inch Uniek QuickShape plastic canvas hexagon
- Uniek Needloft plastic canvas yarn as listed in color key
- Uniek Needloft solid metallic craft cord as listed in color key
- #16 tapestry needle
- 16 (9mm x 6mm) silver pony beads
- 12 (5mm) silver beads
- 172 (3mm) silver beads
- Beading needle
- Transparent thread
- 32 inches 1¼-inch-wide fabric ribbon to match yarn used for poinsettia
- Hot-glue gun

Instructions

1. Cut plastic canvas according to graphs, cutting away gray areas on plastic canvas hexagon, white square on top and white areas at center top and bottom on sides.

2. Stitch and Overcast poinsettia and leaves following graphs. Stitch topper pieces, working Slanted Gobelin Stitches only in center areas, leaving solid silver cord Cross Stitches unworked at this time.

3. Cut fabric ribbon in four 8-inch lengths. For each

side, thread ends of one ribbon length through cutouts along center top and bottom edges; fold ends to wrong side and glue in place to Slanted Gobelin Stitches.

4. Using solid silver cord, work Cross Stitches over ribbon on sides, threading each Cross Stitch through a silver pony bead before completing stitch.

5. Whipstitch sides together with silver yarn. Using beading needle and transparent thread, attach 5mm and 3mm silver beads to sides and poinsettia where indicated on graphs.

6. Using burgundy yarn, Whipstitch sides to top; Overcast bottom edges. Inside edges on top will remain unstitched.

7. Using photo as a guide, glue leaves, then poinsettia to top. ❖

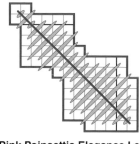

Pink Poinsettia Elegance Leaf
12 holes x 12 holes
Cut 4

COLOR KEY	
Plastic Canvas Yarn	**Yards**
■ Burgundy #03	8
▨ Lavender #05	8
▨ Christmas green #28	4
▨ Silver #37	55
╱ Forest #29 Straight Stitch and Overcasting	4
Solid Metallic Craft Cord	
▨ Solid silver #55021	4
● Attach pony bead	
○ Attach 5mm bead	
● Attach 3mm bead	
Color numbers given are for Uniek Needloft plastic canvas yarn and solid metallic craft cord.	

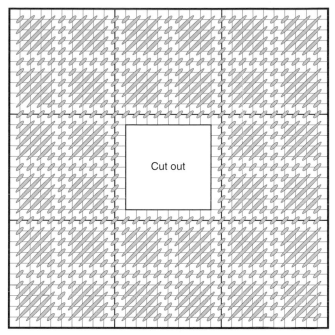

Pink Poinsettia Elegance Top
30 holes x 30 holes
Cut 1

Pink Poinsettia Elegance Poinsettia
Cut 1 from hexagon,
cutting away gray areas

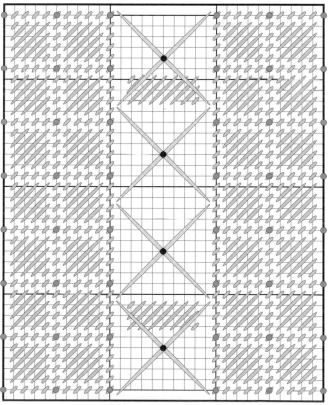

Pink Poinsettia Elegance Side
30 holes x 37 holes
Cut 4

Christmas Holly

Design by Betty Hansen

Blooming boughs of holly and twinkling gold jewels will fill your heart with Christmas joy!

Skill Level: Beginner

Size: Fits boutique-style tissue box

Materials

- 1½ sheets 7-count plastic canvas
- Worsted weight yarn as listed in color key
- Sport weight pompadour yarn as listed in color key
- #16 tapestry needle
- 24 (6mm) gold beads

Project Note

Depending on actual size of boutique-style tissue box, this topper may be a very tight fit.

Instructions

1. Cut plastic canvas according to graphs.

2. Stitch pieces following graphs, working green Double Leviathan Stitches in corners and using 2 strands when stitching with white pompadour yarn.

3. Work French Knots when background stitching is com-pleted, wrapping yarn two times around needle. Use placement of French Knots for holly berries on side graph as a guide, working French Knots as desired.

4. Attach one gold bead in center of each Double Leviathan Stitch using green yarn. Attach one gold bead in center of holly berries on each side using red yarn.

5. Overcast inside edges of top with green, working longer Overcasting Stitches where indicated with a green Straight Stitch symbol.

6. Using red throughout, Overcast bottom edges of sides. Whipstitch sides together, then Whipstitch sides to top. ❖

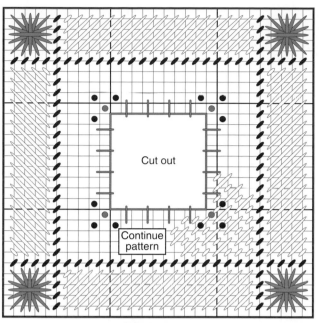

Christmas Holly Top
29 holes x 29 holes
Cut 1

COLOR KEY	
Worsted Weight Yarn	**Yards**
■ Green	25
■ Red	15
■ Burgundy	3
╱ Green Overcasting	
● Red French Knot	
● Burgundy French Knot	
Sport Weight Pompadour Yarn	
☐ White	120

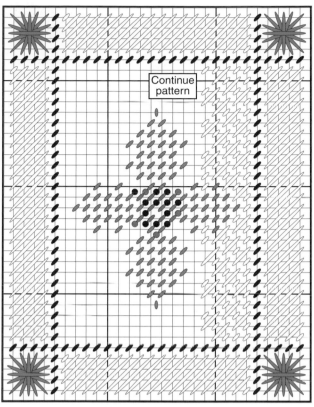

Christmas Holly Side
29 holes x 37 holes
Cut 4

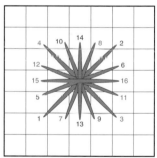

Double Leviathan Stitch

The Gift

Design by Betty Hansen

Ornate ribbons and elegant style make this perfectly wrapped box a gorgeous "gift" for any room in your home!

Skill Level: Beginner

Size: Fits boutique-style tissue box

Materials

- 2 sheets 7-count plastic canvas
- Worsted weight yarn as listed in color key
- Sport weight pompadour yarn as listed in color key
- Metallic yarn as listed in color key
- #16 tapestry needle
- #18 tapestry needle

- Green #3 pearl cotton to match Christmas green glitter yarn
- 92 (6mm) gold beads

Project Note

Depending on actual size of boutique-style tissue box, this topper may be a very tight fit.

Instructions

1. Cut plastic canvas according to graphs.

2. Stitch pieces with #16 tapestry needle following graphs. When background stitching is completed,

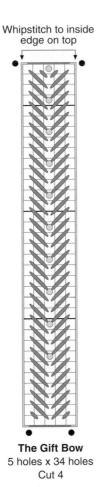

Whipstitch to inside edge on top

The Gift Bow
5 holes x 34 holes
Cut 4

COLOR KEY	
Worsted Weight Yarn	**Yards**
■ Christmas green glitter	30
■ Red	25
Sport Weight Pompadour Yarn	
□ White	25
Metallic Yarn	
□ Gold	15
○ Attach gold bead	

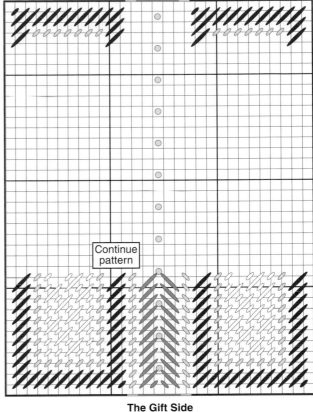

The Gift Side
29 holes x 37 holes
Cut 4

Continue pattern

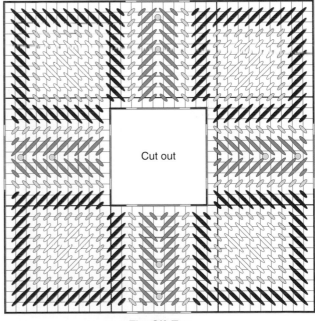

Cut out

The Gift Top
29 holes x 29 holes
Cut 1

attach gold beads where indicated using green pearl cotton and #18 tapestry needle.

3. Using gold yarn, Overcast long edges of bows around bottom corners from black dot to black dot. Whipstitch short end indicated on bows to inside edges of top with Christmas green glitter and gold; Overcast corners of opening on top with red.

4. Using Christmas green glitter yarn, tack remaining short end of each bow to top along blue lines.

5. Following graphs, Whipstitch sides together, then Whipstitch sides to top. Overcast bottom edges. ❖

Santa's Workshop

Design by Angie Arickx

Candy canes and gingerbread sweeten the appeal of this delectable Christmas confection!

Skill Level: Intermediate

Size: Fits boutique-style tissue box

Materials
- 2 sheets 7-count plastic canvas
- Uniek Needloft plastic canvas yarn as listed in color key

- 6-strand embroidery floss as listed in color key
- #16 tapestry needle
- Hot-glue gun

Instructions

1. Cut plastic canvas according to graphs (pages 167 and 168).

COLOR KEY

Plastic Canvas Yarn	Yards
■ Christmas red #02	21
■ Maple #13	4
■ Holly #27	61
□ White #41	54
□ Yellow #57	6
Uncoded area on signs are Christmas red #02 Continental Stitches	
⁄ White #41 Backstitch	
● Black #00 French Knot	1
6-Strand Embroidery Floss	
⁄ Black Backstitch and Straight Stitch	3

Color numbers given are for Uniek Needloft plastic canvas yarn.

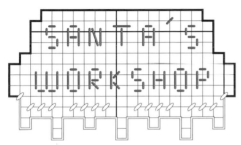

Santa's Workshop Sign
21 holes x 12 holes
Cut 2

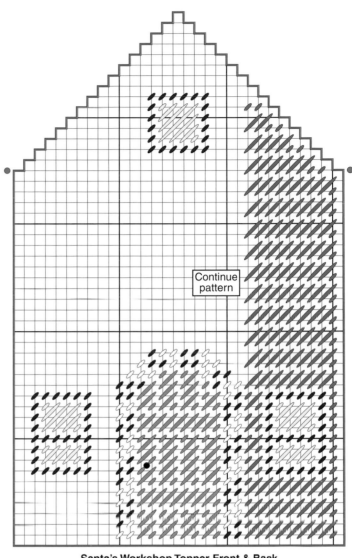

Continue pattern

Santa's Workshop Topper Front & Back
31 holes x 50 holes
Cut 2

2. Stitch and Overcast icicles and signs following graphs, working uncoded areas on signs with red Continental Stitches. Stitch all remaining pieces.

3. When background stitching is completed, use white yarn to work Backstitches on chimney sides, black yarn to work French Knot on each door and black floss to work lettering on signs.

4. Using holly throughout, Overcast bottom edges of topper front, back and sides. Overcast top edges of topper sides and top edges of front and back from blue dot to blue dot. Whipstitch front and back to sides.

5. Using white through step 6, Overcast bottom edges of roof sides and vertical edges of chimney openings on roof sides; Overcast bottom edges of eaves from arrow to arrow.

6. Whipstitch chimney sides together. Whipstitch top edges of roof sides together, then Whipstitch bottom edges of two chimney sides to horizontal edges of chimney opening. **Note:** *The last two bottom edges of chimney sides will remain unstitched.* Whipstitch eaves to roof sides.

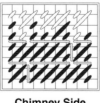

Chimney Side
9 holes x 8 holes
Cut 4

Santa's Workshop Icicle
7 holes x 3 holes
Cut 18

7. Glue one icicle under each window; glue one sign above each door (see photo). Place roof on topper sides; secure with glue. ❖

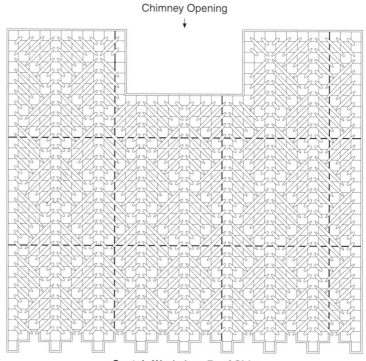

Santa's Workshop Roof Eave
30 holes x 30 holes
Cut 2

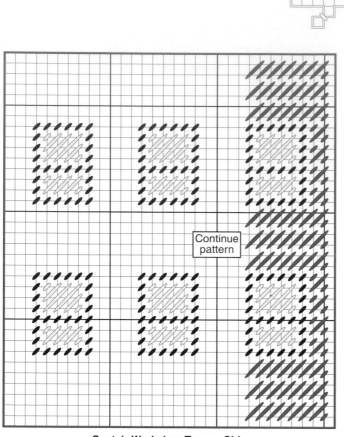

Santa's Workshop Topper Side
31 holes x 35 holes
Cut 2

COLOR KEY

Plastic Canvas Yarn	Yards
■ Christmas red #02	21
■ Maple #13	4
■ Holly #27	61
□ White #41	54
□ Yellow #57	6
Uncoded area on signs are Christmas red #02 Continental Stitches	
╱ White #41 Backstitch	
● Black #00 French Knot	1
6-Strand Embroidery Floss	
╱ Black Backstitch and Straight Stitch	3

Color numbers given are for Uniek Needloft plastic canvas yarn.

Chimney Opening

Santa's Workshop Roof Side
33 holes x 30 holes
Cut 2

Believe

Design by Kathy Wirth

Full of irresistible Christmas magic, this charming topper-and-ornament
set will have all your holiday guests believing in Santa Claus!

Skill Level: Intermediate

Size: Fits regular-size tissue box

Materials

- 1 1/2 sheets clear stiff 7-count plastic canvas
- 1/2 sheet white 10-count plastic canvas
- DMC #3 pearl cotton as listed in color key
- #16 tapestry needle
- #20 tapestry needle
- 7 (22mm) amber acrylic faceted stars
- Wedge makeup sponge
- Hot-glue gun

Project Notes

Use 2 strands pearl cotton and #16 tapestry needle

to stitch sides, ends and top, making sure stitches lie flat and untwisted.

Use 1 strand pearl cotton and #20 tapestry needle to stitch Santas.

To cut pearl cotton skeins into 15 lengths approximately 1 yard each in length, remove wrappers, open skein and untwist to form loop; cut through thread that holds strands together; then cut through all strands at same point, cutting off knot.

Topper

1. Cut top, sides and ends from stiff 7-count plastic canvas according to graphs (pages 170, 171 and 172).

2. Stitch top following project notes and graph, working uncoded areas with very dark royal blue

Continental Stitches. Work very dark royal blue Straight Stitches only in corners; do not work Continental Stitches under them.

3. Stitch sides and ends following project notes and graphs, working uncoded areas with white Continental Stitches and using 1 strand each of bright green and chartreuse in same needle to work trees, keeping chartreuse at top. Leave area shaded with blue unworked on one side only.

4. When background stitching is completed, work bright red Straight Stitches to complete "Vs." Work medium light topaz Straight Stitches between words. Straight Stitch tree trunks, using 1 strand each of bright green and chartreuse in same needle.

5. Following graphs, Overcast inside edges of top and bottom edges of sides. Whipstitch sides to ends, then Whipstitch sides and ends to top.

Santas

1. Cut Santas from white 10-count plastic canvas according to graph (page 171).

2. Stitch Santas following graph, working very dark royal blue French Knots for eyes and bright red Backstitches for mouth. Do not Overcast.

Finishing

1. Glue one amber star to unstitched portion on right side of each Santa's hat.

2. For ornament hanger, attach desired length of bright red pearl cotton to center top of one Santa with a Lark's Head Knot.

COLOR KEY	
#3 Pearl Cotton	**Yards**
☐ White	75
■ Bright red #666	25
■ Bright green #700	23
☐ Chartreuse #703	23
☐ Bright green #700 and chartreuse #703 combined	
☐ Medium light topaz #725	3
■ Very dark royal blue #820	104
☐ Very light peach #948	1
Uncoded areas on sides and ends are white Continental Stitches	
Uncoded areas on top are very dark royal blue #820 Continental Stitches	
✓ Bright red #666 Backstitch and Straight Stitch	
⁄ Bright green #700 and chartreuse #703 Straight Stitch	
⁄ Medium light topaz #725 Straight Stitch	
✓ Very dark royal blue #820 Straight Stitch	
● Very dark royal blue #820 French Knot	
Color numbers given are for DMC #3 pearl cotton.	

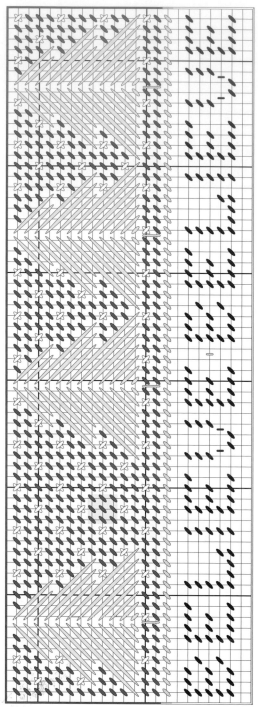

Believe Side
65 holes x 23 holes
Cut 2 from stiff 7-count

3. Cut ³/₈-inch cube from makeup sponge. Glue sponge to unworked blue shaded area on one side. Center remaining Santa over sponge and glue in place at a slight angle (see photo). Glue one amber star between first two trees on remaining side.

4. Glue one star just above letter "I" in word "BELIEVE" on each end and above letter "I" in second word "BELIEVE" on both sides. ❖

COLOR KEY

#3 Pearl Cotton	Yards
☐ White	75
■ Bright red #666	25
■ Bright green #700	23
☐ Chartreuse #703	23
☐ Bright green #700 and chartreuse #703 combined	
☐ Medium light topaz #725	3
■ Very dark royal blue #820	104
☐ Very light peach #948	1

Uncoded areas on sides and ends
are white Continental Stitches
Uncoded areas on top are very dark
royal blue #820 Continental Stitches
⁄ Bright red #666 Backstitch
and Straight Stitch
⁄ Bright green #700 and
chartreuse #703 Straight Stitch
⁄ Medium light topaz #725 Straight Stitch
⁄ Very dark royal blue #820 Straight Stitch
● Very dark royal blue #820 French Knot
Color numbers given are for DMC #3 pearl cotton.

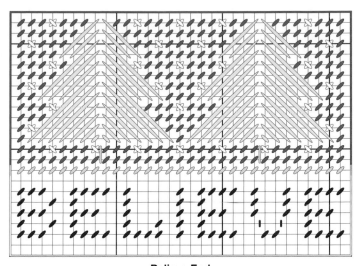

Believe End
32 holes x 23 holes
Cut 2 from stiff 7-count

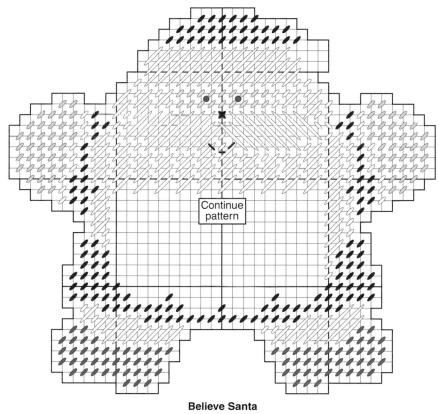

Believe Santa
40 holes x 36 holes
Cut 2 from white 10-count

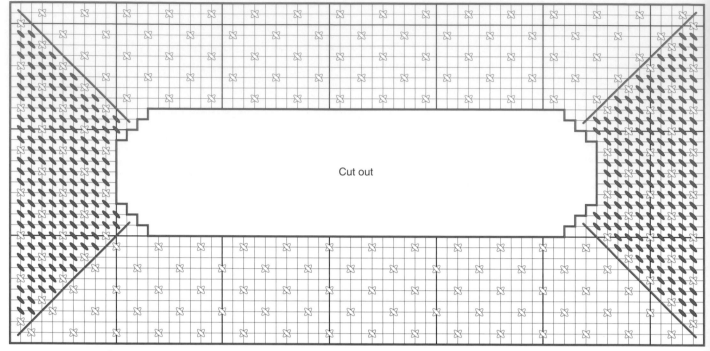

Believe Top
65 holes x 32 holes
Cut 1 from stiff 7-count

COLOR KEY	
#3 Pearl Cotton	**Yards**
☐ White	75
■ Bright red #666	25
■ Bright green #700	23
☐ Chartreuse #703	23
☐ Bright green #700 and chartreuse #703 combined	
☐ Medium light topaz #725	3
■ Very dark royal blue #820	104
☐ Very light peach #948	1
Uncoded areas on sides and ends are white Continental Stitches	
Uncoded areas on top are very dark royal blue #820 Continental Stitches	
╱ Bright red #666 Backstitch and Straight Stitch	
╱ Bright green #700 and chartreuse #703 Straight Stitch	
╱ Medium light topaz #725 Straight Stitch	
╱ Very dark royal blue #820 Straight Stitch	
● Very dark royal blue #820 French Knot	
Color numbers given are for DMC #3 pearl cotton.	

Special Thanks

We would like to acknowledge and thank the following designers whose original work has been published in this collection. We appreciate and value their creativity and dedication to designing quality plastic canvas projects!

Debra Arch
Pretty in Pink Kitty

Angie Arickx
Apple Delight, County Star Quilt, Diagonal Weave, End Table Organizer, English Cottage, Old Glory Quilt Block, Patchwork Pinwheels, Poinsettia Patchwork, Santa's Workshop, White Roses on Amethyst

Kathy Barwick
Victorian Elegance

Ronda Bryce
Missing Pieces, My Favorite Pair of Jeans, My Favorite Things

Mary T. Cosgrove
Fantasy Tree

Janelle Giese
Egret Bay, Elegant Fruit Basket, Garden Bees, Kitty Chef, Sea Treasures, Silver Filigree, To Market, Skateboard Pup, Tutu Bear

Betty Hansen
Christmas Holly, Floral Surprise, The Gift

Kathleen Hurley
Tropical Treat

Barbara Ivie
New Mexico

Nancy Knapp
Satin & Gold

Susan Leinberger
Cosmetics Caddy, Cross Stitch Fantasy, Pink Poinsettia Elegance, Sweet Sunflower

Kristine Loffredo
Tribal Motif, Woven Lattice

Alida Macor
Pastel Patchwork

Maryanne Moreck
Baby's Garden, Christmas Sophistication, Elegant Plaid, Goldfish Bowl

Terry Ricioli
Leafy Glade

Cynthia Roberts
A Spot of Tea, Red Toile

Kimberly A. Suber
Happy Faces, Southwestern Quilt, Sunflower Gingham

Ruby Thacker
Sea Horse Duo, Southwest Quilt Block, Study in Blue

Kathy Wirth
Art Deco, Believe, Checks & Cherries, Daisies on Blue, God Bless This Home, Golden Diamonds, Gold Ribbon, Heart Swirls, Holiday Wonderland, Just Ducky, Noel, Ruler of the Roost, Squares in Squares, Stack-n-Stitch Jewel Tone, Stenciled Flowers, Stylized Flowers

Buyer's Guide

When looking for a specific material, first check your local craft and retail stores. If you are unable to locate a product locally, contact the manufacturers listed below for the closest retail source in your area or a mail-order source.

Amaco
American Art Clay Co. Inc.,
4717 W. 16th St., Indianapolis, IN
46222-2598 (317) 244-6871
www.amaco.com

The Beadery
P.O. Box 178, Hope Valley, RI 02832
(401) 539-2432
www.thebeadery.com

C.M. Offray & Son Inc./Lion Ribbon Co. Inc.
Rte. 24, Box 601, Chester, NJ 07930
(800) 551-LION
www.offray.com

Coats & Clark Inc.
Consumer Service
P.O. Box 12229, Greenville, SC
29612-0229, (800) 648-1479
www.coatsandclark.com

Darice
Mail-order source:

Schrock's International
P.O. Box 538, Bolivar, OH 44612,
(330) 874-3700

DMC Corp.
Hackensack Ave. Bldg. 10A, South
Kearny, NJ 07032-4688, (800) 275-4117
www.dmc-usa.com

Elmore-Pisgah Inc.
204 Oak St., Spindale, NC 28160
(800) 633-7829
www.elmore-pisgah.com

Gay Bowles Sales Inc.
P.O. Box 1060, Janesville, WI 53547
(800) 447-1332
www.millhill.com

Kreinik Mfg. Co. Inc.
3106 Lord Baltimore Dr. #101,
Baltimore, MD 21244-2871
(800) 537-2166
www.kreinik.com

Kunin Felt Co./Foss Mfg. Co. Inc.
P.O. Box 5000, Hampton, NH
03843-5000, (603) 929-6100
www.kuninfelt.com

Lion Brand Yarn Co.
34 W. 15th St., New York, NY 10011
(800) 258-9276
www.lionbrand.com

Madeira Threads
For dealer in your area, call:
(800) 542-8025

Rainbow Gallery
7412 Fulton Ave., #5, North Hollywood,
CA 91605-4126, (818) 982-4496
www.rainbowgallery.com

Uniek
Mail-order source:

Annie's Attic
1 Annie Ln., Big Sandy, TX 75755
(800) 582-6643
www.anniesattic.com

Stitch Guide

Use the following diagrams to expand your plastic canvas stitching skills. For each diagram, bring needle up through canvas at the red number one and go back down through the canvas at the red number two. The second stitch is numbered in green. Always bring needle up through the canvas at odd numbers and take it back down through the canvas at the even numbers.

Background Stitches

The following stitches are used for filling in large areas of canvas. The Continental Stitch is the most commonly used stitch. Other stitches, such as the Condensed Mosaic and Scotch Stitch, fill in large areas of canvas more quickly than the Continental Stitch because their stitches cover a larger area of canvas.

Continental Stitch

Condensed Mosaic

Alternating Continental

Cross Stitch

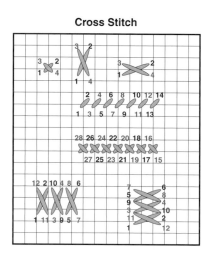

Long Stitch

Scotch Stitch

Slanted Gobelin

Embroidery Stitches

These stitches are worked on top of a stitched area to add detail to the project. Embroidery stitches are usually worked with one strand of yarn, several strands of pearl cotton or several strands of embroidery floss.

Lattice Stitch

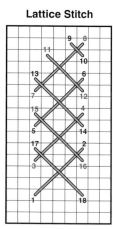

Chain Stitch

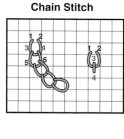

Couching

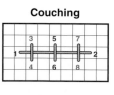

Straight Stitch

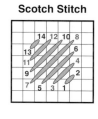

Running Stitch

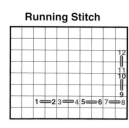

Fly Stitch

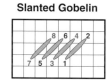

Backstitch

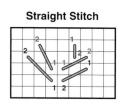

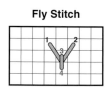

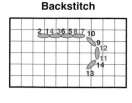

Embroidery Stitches

French Knot

Bring needle up through canvas.

Wrap yarn around needle 1 to 3 times, depending on desired size of knot; take needle back through canvas through same hole.

Lazy Daisy

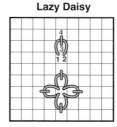

Loop Stitch/Turkey Loop Stitch

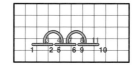

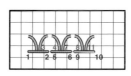

Bring yarn needle up through canvas, then back down in same hole, leaving a small loop.

Then, bring needle up inside loop; take needle back down through canvas on other side of loop.

The top diagram shows this stitch left intact. This is an effective stitch for giving a project dimensional hair. The bottom diagram demonstrates the cut loop stitch. Because each stitch is anchored, cutting it will not cause the stitches to come out. A group of cut loop stitches gives a fluffy, soft look and feel to your project.

Specialty Stitches

The following stitches can be worked either on top of a previously stitched area or directly onto the canvas. Like the embroidery stitches, these too add wonderful detail and give your stitching additional interest and texture.

Diamond Eyelet

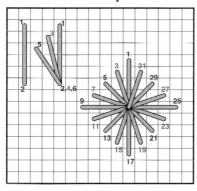

For each stitch, bring needle up at odd numbers and down through canvas at center hole.

Smyrna Cross

Satin Stitches

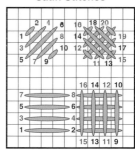

Finishing Stitches

Overcast/Whipstitch

Overcasting and Whipstitching are used to finish the outer edges of the canvas. Overcasting is done to finish one edge at a time. Whipstitching is used to stitch two or more pieces of canvas together along an edge. For both Overcasting and Whipstitching, work one stitch in each hole along straight edges and inside corners, and two or three stitches in outside corners.

Lark's Head Knot

The Lark's Head Knot is used for a fringe edge or for attaching a hanging loop.